Volume equivalents

IMPERIAL	METRIC	IMPERIAL	METRIC
1fl oz	30ml	15fl oz	450ml
2fl oz	60ml	16fl oz	500ml
2½fl oz	75ml	2 cups	500ml
3½fl oz	100ml	1 pint	500ml
4fl oz	120ml	3 cups	700ml
5fl oz	150ml	4 cups	950ml
6fl oz	175ml	2 pints	950ml
7fl oz	200ml	2 pints	roughly 1 liter
8fl oz	250ml	2½ pints	1.2 liters
10fl oz	300ml	3 pints	1.4 liters
12fl oz	350ml	3½ pints	1.7 liters
14fl oz	400ml	4 pints	1.8 liters

Weight equivalents

IMPERIAL	METRIC	IMPERIAL	METRIC
½oz	15g	5½oz	150g
¾oz	20g	6oz	175g
scant 1oz	25g	7oz	200g
1oz	30g	8oz	225g
1½oz	45g	9oz	250g
1⅓oz	50g	10oz	300g
2oz	60g	1lb	450g
2½oz	75g	1lb 2oz	500g
3oz	85g	1½lb	675g
3½oz	100g	2lb	900g
4oz	115g	2¼lb	1kg
4½oz	125g	3lb 3oz	1.5kg
5oz	140g	4lb	1.8kg

everyday
easy
One-pot

Based on content previously published in
The Illustrated Kitchen Bible

everyday easy
One-pot

hearty soups • quick stir-fries • simple casseroles

DK

LONDON, NEW YORK, MELBOURNE,
MUNICH, AND DELHI

US Editor
Kate Johnsen

Editor
Andrew Roff

Designer
Kathryn Wilding

Senior Jacket Creative
Nicola Powling

Managing Editor
Dawn Henderson

Managing Art Editor
Christine Keilty

Production Editor
Ben Marcus

Production Controller
Hema Gohil

Creative Technical Support
Sonia Charbonnier

DK INDIA

Head of Publishing
Aparna Sharma

Design Manager
Romi Chakraborty

Designer
Neha Ahuja

DTP Coordinator
Balwant Singh

DTP Designer
Tarun Sharma

Material first published in *The Illustrated Kitchen Bible* in 2008
This edition first published in the United States
by DK Publishing, 375 Hudson Street
New York, New York 10014

10 11 12   10 9 8 7 6 5 4 3 2

176449—October 2009

A catalog record for this book is available from the Library of Congress.

ISBN 978-0-7566-5793-2

DK books are available at special discounts when purchased in bulk for
sales promotions, premiums, fund-raising, or educational use. For details,
contact: DK Publishing Special Markets, 375 Hudson Street, New York,
New York 10014 or SpecialSales@dk.com.

Color reproduction by MDP, Bath, UK
Printed and bound in Singapore by Star Standard

Discover more at
www.dk.com

CONTENTS

Soups, stews, casseroles, stir-fries—all delicious and all require just one pot to make. Cooking all the ingredients in a pot allows their flavors to mingle, infuse, and develop, making one-pot meals some of the tastiest. A one-pot recipe may involve another pan or bowl to brown meat, fry onions, or whip eggs but all the components finally meet in one pot to produce something good. Bring the pot to the kitchen table, lift the lid, and enjoy.

As well as the superb taste, one-pot meals have many practical benefits— spend time doing something else while your pot bubbles away in the oven or on the stove, enjoy your meal without the thought of the dishes waiting for you (with just one pot, there won't be many!), and easily divide the contents of the pot for the people you need to feed or save any leftovers for tomorrow's lunch.

The popularity of one-pot cooking is far and wide. Some of the world's best-loved dishes involve slow-cooking in one pot—Chili Con Carne, Irish Stew, and Osso Bucco are prime examples. Other one-pot recipes seem exotic and adventurous but are just as simple to make—Kedgeree and Pad Thai require the bare minimum of equipment and hardly any cooking. Whatever you like, the recipes on the following pages won't disappoint.

The book begins with a selection of step-by-step **Techniques** that will refine your core cooking skills. Properly done, these techniques will cut your preparation time in half and ensure you get the most from your ingredients. Some techniques are simple, those kitchen tasks involved in many recipes, such as peeling and chopping garlic and dicing an onion. Other techniques are more specialized, revealing the secrets to perfect pasta, stir-fried vegetables, and fresh tomato sauce.

Six **Recipe Planners** follow—photos that showcase recipes so you can quickly find something that sounds appetizing. Organized according to key ingredient, these are perfect if you are craving fish, pasta, meat, legumes, or chicken, for example.

The first recipes use common kitchen ingredients or everyday items that you would pick up on your weekly grocery trip. This **Budget** section will produce impressive, nutritious family food without great expense. Macaroni and Three Cheeses and Tuna and Pasta Bake are particular family favorites that cost very little to make.

Next comes the **Hearty** section. Beans and other legumes can be loaded with a variety of flavors and make for hearty food that is perfect for satisfying hunger pangs. Serve these meals, such as Tuscan Bean Soup and Vegetable Biryani, in bowls and leave plenty in the pot, simmering on the stove, so the family can return for seconds (and probably thirds) when they want to—great for cold winter evenings.

After a busy day, turn to the **Super Quick** section where you'll find a collection of recipes you can transform from ingredients to meal in minutes. Singapore Noodles and Thai Green Chicken Curry are favorite recipes that you can create in moments.

Choose something low in fat or GI (Glycemic Index) from the **Healthy** section, packed with tantalizing recipes that you can proudly feed to your family. With such delights as Spaghetti Mare e Monti and Swordfish Baked with Herbs, these recipes are as irresistible as they are nutritious.

Lastly, you'll find a selection of recipes that will be a treat when entertaining. Bouillabaisse and Mussels in White Wine Sauce are simple to prepare and guarantee to **Impress**. And what could be better for you as the host when entertaining than a one-pot recipe? Enjoy a glass of wine with your friends as your meal cooks away in the kitchen. Many one-pot meals won't be ruined by a few extra minutes cooking so you can serve your food when you're ready for it.

One-pot meals are designed to be shared. Put the pot on the kitchen table and let the family help themselves—a dinnertime ritual to bring everyone together to enjoy great food.

A guide to symbols

The recipes in this book are accompanied by symbols that alert you to important information.

 Tells you how many people the recipe serves, or the quantity.

 Indicates how much time you will need to prepare and cook a dish. Next to this symbol you will also find out if additional time is required for such things as marinating, standing, or cooling. You will have to read the recipe to find out exactly how much extra time is needed.

 Points out nutritional benefits, such as low fat or low GI (Glycemic Index).

 This important alert refers to preparation work that must be done before you can begin to cook the recipe. For example, you may need to soak some beans overnight.

 This denotes that special equipment is required, such as an oven-proof pot or skewers. Where possible, alternatives are given.

 This symbol accompanies freezing information.

Oven temperature equivalents

FAHRENHEIT	CELSIUS	DESCRIPTION
225°F	110°C	Cool
250°F	130°C	Cool
275°F	140°C	Very low
300°F	150°C	Very low
325°F	160°C	Low
350°F	180°C	Moderate
375°F	190°C	Moderately hot
400°F	200°C	Hot
425°F	220°C	Hot
450°F	230°C	Very hot
475°F	240°C	Very hot

Refrigerator and freezer storage guide

FOOD	REFRIGERATOR	FREEZER
Raw poultry, fish, and meat (small pieces)	2–3 days	3–6 months
Raw ground beef and poultry	1–2 days	3 months
Cooked whole roasts or whole poultry	2–3 days	9 months
Cooked poultry pieces	1–2 days	1 month (6 months in stock or gravy)
Soups and stews	2–3 days	1–3 months
Casseroles	2–3 days	2–4 weeks

Volume equivalents

IMPERIAL	METRIC	IMPERIAL	METRIC
1fl oz	30ml	10fl oz	300ml
2fl oz	60ml	12fl oz	350ml
2$\frac{1}{2}$fl oz	75ml	14fl oz	400ml
3$\frac{1}{2}$fl oz	100ml	15fl oz	450ml
4fl oz	120ml	16fl oz	500ml
5fl oz	150ml	2 cups	500ml
6fl oz	175ml	1 pint	500ml
7fl oz	200ml	4 cups	950ml
8fl oz	250ml	2 pints	roughly 1 liter

Weight equivalents

IMPERIAL	METRIC	IMPERIAL	METRIC
scant 1oz	25g	4$\frac{1}{2}$oz	125g
1oz	30g	5oz	140g
1$\frac{1}{2}$oz	45g	5$\frac{1}{2}$oz	150g
1$\frac{1}{3}$oz	50g	6oz	175g
2oz	60g	7oz	200g
2$\frac{1}{2}$oz	75g	8oz	225g
3oz	85g	9oz	250g
3$\frac{1}{2}$oz	100g	1lb	450g
4oz	115g	2$\frac{1}{4}$lb	1kg

TECHNIQUES

Peel and chop garlic

Garlic is used in many recipes and peeling it is easy once you know how.
The finer you chop garlic, the more flavor you'll release.

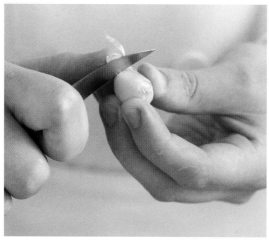

1 Lay each garlic clove flat on a cutting board. Place the side of a chef's knife blade on it. Lightly strike the blade to break the skin. Peel and discard the skin and cut the ends off from each clove.

2 Chop the garlic roughly, then sprinkle with a little salt to prevent it from sticking to the knife. Continue chopping as necessary.

Dice an onion

Once an onion is cut in half, it can be sliced or diced. This technique is for quick dicing, which helps keep your eyes from watering.

1 Using a sharp knife, cut the onion lengthwise in half and peel. Lay one half flat side down. Make a few slices into the onion horizontally, cutting up to the root, then slice down vertically, cutting up to the root.

2 Cut across the vertical slices to produce even dice. Use the root to hold the onion steady, then discard when the onion is diced.

Seed and cut chilies

Chilies contain capsaicin, a pungent compound that is a strong irritant to skin and mucus membranes.

1 Cut the chili lengthwise in half. Using the tip of your knife or a small spoon, scrape out and discard the seeds, ribs, and stem.

2 Flatten each chili half with the palm of your hand, and slice lengthwise into strips. For dice, hold the strips firmly together and slice crosswise.

Prepare bell peppers

Red, green, orange, and yellow peppers add their brilliant color and sweetness to stir-fries and distinctive flavor to many dishes.

1 Place the pepper on its side and cut off the top and bottom. Stand the pepper on one of the cut ends, and slice it in half lengthwise. Remove the core and seeds.

2 Open each section and lay flat on the cutting board. Sliding the knife sideways, remove the remaining pale, fleshy ribs. Cut the peppers into sections, following the divisions of the pepper.

Peel and seed tomatoes

When using tomatoes in sauces and soups, they are often peeled and seeded. Prepare your tomatoes by removing the stem, then score an "X" at their base.

1 Immerse the tomato in a pan of boiling water for 20 seconds. With a slotted spoon, remove the tomato and submerge it in a bowl of ice water.

2 When cool enough to handle, use a paring knife to peel away the loosened skin. Cut each tomato in half and gently squeeze out the seeds.

Make fresh tomato sauce

This simple, yet versatile, sauce is perfect with fish, poultry, meat, and vegetables. This recipe makes 2½ cups. Reheat thoroughly before serving.

In a saucepan over low heat, place 2 tbsp unsalted butter, 2 chopped shallots, 1 tbsp olive oil, 1 bay leaf, and 3 crushed garlic cloves. Cover and sweat for 5–6 minutes until shallots are soft, but not brown. Seed and chop 2¼lb (1kg) ripe plum tomatoes, and add them to the pan with 2 tbsp tomato paste and 1 tbsp sugar. Cook uncovered for 5 minutes, then add 1 cup water and bring to a boil. Reduce the heat, and simmer for 30 minutes, then season to taste with salt and pepper. Using a ladle, press the sauce through a sieve and serve.

Chop herbs

Chop fresh herbs just before using to release their flavor and aroma. Reserve a small amount to use as a garnish for the finished dish if you wish.

1 To chop leaves (a mixture or a single variety as the basil leaves above), gather them together, and roll them up tightly.

2 Using a large, sharp knife, chop through the herbs, using a steady rocking motion, turning the pile 90° until you have the size you want.

Stir-fry

This cooking method uses very little oil, so the vegetables retain their natural flavors and take hardly any time to cook.

1 Heat the wok or pan and add the oil (sunflower, canola, or peanut), tilting the pan to spread the oil around the base. When very hot, add flavorings, such as garlic, ginger, chili, or scallions, and quickly toss.

2 Add the desired vegetables and toss, moving them from the center to the sides. When stir-frying vegetables, such as broccoli, add a little water and cover. Cook until the vegetables are tender and crisp.

Chicken or meat stock

By simmering the remains of your roast with a few vegetables and herbs, you can produce a stock from scratch for soups and risottos.

1 Add either raw chicken bones or roasted meat bones into a large stockpot with carrots, celery, onions, and a bouquet garni of fresh herbs. Add water and bring to the boil.

2 Simmer for 1–3 hours, skimming frequently. Ladle through a fine sieve and season to taste. Let cool and refrigerate for up to 2 days. Lift any congealed fat from the surface with a slotted spoon.

Vegetable stock

Simmering water with vegetables will capture their delicate flavor. Use the stock to flavor soups and risottos when preparing vegetarian meals.

1 Place chopped carrots, celery, onion, and leeks into a large stockpot. Add peppercorns, parsley, and bay leaves. Cover with water and bring to a boil. Reduce the heat and simmer for up to 1 hour.

2 Ladle through a fine sieve, pressing the vegetables against the sieve to extract any extra liquid. Season to taste with salt and freshly ground black pepper, let cool, and refrigerate for up to 2 days.

Fish stock

Keep the parts of your fish you don't use in cooking to make a stock—perfect for using in seafood soups and stews.

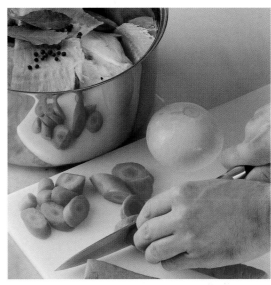

1 Using a sharp knife, cut the bones and trimmings of non-oily, mild fish into equal pieces. Rinse in plenty of cold water to remove the blood. Drain, and place the bones and trimmings into a large stockpot.

2 Cut carrots, celery, and onion into equal-sized pieces, and add them (and any other flavorings you wish), into the pan with the fish. Cover with water, increase the heat, and bring to a boil.

3 Once the stock reaches a boil, lower the heat, and simmer for 20 minutes (any longer and the stock will start to become bitter). Skim off the scum that rises to the surface with a slotted spoon.

4 Ladle through a fine sieve, pressing the solids against the sieve to extract any extra liquid. Season to taste with salt and freshly ground black pepper, let cool, and refrigerate for up to 3 days.

Cook rice by absorption

In the West, packaged rice is thoroughly cleaned, so soaking it before cooking will only wash away the nutrients. Use 1¹/₂ times as much water or stock as rice.

Put the rice and liquid into a large saucepan. Bring to a boil over medium heat, stir once, and lower the heat to simmer uncovered for 10–12 minutes, or until all, or almost all, the liquid is absorbed. Remove the saucepan from the heat and cover with a clean, folded towel and a tight-fitting lid. Return to the lowest heat and leave the rice to steam, without removing the lid, for 10 minutes. Remove the folded towel and replace the lid. Leave the rice to sit for 5 minutes, covered with the lid. Uncover, fluff the rice with a fork, and serve.

Boil noodles

Most Asian noodles are boiled for a few minutes before using; rice noodles only need to be soaked in boiling water.

1 To boil Asian-style noodles, bring a large saucepan of water to a rolling boil. Add the noodles, allow the water to return to a boil, then cook until the noodles are softened and pliable, about 2 minutes.

2 Drain the noodles in a strainer. Refresh under cold running water to prevent them from cooking further, then drain. Toss the noodles with a little oil and use immediately or proceed with a recipe.

Cook dried pasta

Keep dried pasta on hand, as it is the start of many quick dishes. It is very simple to make but all too easy to overcook.

1 Bring a large pan of salted water to a rapid boil, and gently pour in the pasta. Stir well. Boil uncovered, using the recommended cooking time on the package as a guide, until *al dente*.

2 As soon as the pasta is *al dente*, quickly drain the pasta by pouring it into a large colander, shaking it gently to remove any excess water. Toss the pasta with a little oil and serve or proceed with the recipe.

Make couscous

With no cooking on the stove or in the oven, couscous has to be the easiest and fastest side dish there is. Use around 1³/₄ times as much water as couscous.

1 Pour quick-cook couscous and a pinch of salt into a large bowl and pour over boiling water. Cover with a folded dish towel, leave for 5 minutes, remove the dish towel, and fluff up with a fork.

2 Re-cover the bowl and leave for another 5 minutes. Remove the dish towel and add either 1 tbsp of olive oil or unsalted butter, and fluff up the couscous until light. Serve.

Pasta and noodles

Spaghetti mare e monti
page 160

Tuna and pasta bake page 44

Pappardelle with ragù page 68

Stracciatella with pasta page 120

Pad Thai page 72

Macaroni bake with ham and peppers page 70

Mediterranean lasagna page 184

Thai noodle stir-fry page 48

Singapore noodles page 124

Spaghetti with puttanesca
page 50

Fideua page 164

Pasta alla carbonara page 122

Legumes, rice, and grains

Puy lentils with goat cheese, olives, and fresh thyme page 128

Quinoa tabbouleh page 126

Minestrone page 40

Hoppin' John page 96

Vegetable biryani page 78

Lentil salad with lemon and almonds page 156

Kasha with vegetables page 158

Kedgeree page 76

Arroz con pollo page 172

Chicken and chickpea pilaf page 168

Seafood paella page 188

23

Vegetarian

Mushroom soup page 34

Tofu and mushroom stroganoff page 46

Curried parsnip soup page 36

Porcini mushroom soup page 60

Macaroni and three cheeses page 54

Vegetable curry page 74

Vegetable biryani page 78

Watercress and pear soup page 118

Quinoa tabbouleh page 126

Puy lentils with goat cheese, olives, and fresh thyme page 128

Tomato soup page 150

Kasha with vegetables page 158

Lentil soup page 154

Lentil salad with lemon and almonds page 156

Carrot and orange soup page 152

Chili tofu stir-fry page 162

Winter vegetable soup page 42

Mediterranean lasagna page 184

Fish and shellfish

Herb-baked swordfish page 166

New England clam chowder page 64

Sweet and sour shrimp page 80

Shrimp diablo page 82

Seafood paella page 188

Cod in tomato sauce page 86

Finnan haddie with spinach and pancetta page 132

Seafood curry page 134

Fisherman's tuna stew page 182

Baked porgy page 200

Shellfish and tomato stew page 84

Mussels in white wine sauce page 190

Mussels with spicy tomato sauce page 198

Salt cod braised with vegetables page 196

Bouillabaisse page 180

27

Poultry and game

Chicken gumbo page 204

Chicken paprikash page 88

Thai green chicken curry page 136

Pot roast of guinea hen with cabbage and walnuts page 94

Arroz con pollo page 172

Singapore noodles page 124

Grilled quail with ginger glaze page 206

Chicken stew with herb dumplings page 92

Creamy tarragon chicken page 90

Chicken and chickpea pilaf page 168

Meat

Pork and leek pie page 52

Hoppin' John page 96

Braised lamb page 104

Roast lamb with white beans page 100

Lamb tagine with couscous page 102

Navarin of lamb page 106

Meat loaf page 114

Thai red beef curry page 110

Irish stew page 108

Quick lamb curry page 140

Chinese chili beef stir-fry page 142

Daube beef with wild mushrooms page 210

Veal scaloppine page 212

Beef stroganoff page 208

Choucroute garni page 214

Osso bucco page 216

Mushroom soup

Using a selection of both wild and cultivated mushrooms will produce a soup that is bursting with flavor.

INGREDIENTS
2 tbsp butter
1 onion, finely chopped
2 celery ribs, finely chopped
1 garlic clove, crushed
1lb (450g) mixed mushrooms,
   cleaned and coarsely chopped
1 quart vegetable or chicken stock
7oz (200g) baking potatoes, peeled and cubed
2 tbsp finely chopped parsley
salt and freshly ground black pepper

METHOD
1 Melt the butter in a large saucepan over medium heat. Add the onion, celery, and garlic and cook for about 3–4 minutes, or until softened.

2 Stir in the mushrooms and cook for 5–6 minutes more. Add the stock and potatoes and bring to a boil. Reduce the heat and simmer gently for 30 minutes.

3 In batches, process in a blender or food processor with the lid ajar until coarsely puréed.

4 Sprinkle in the parsley and season with salt and pepper. Serve hot.

GOOD WITH Warm crusty rolls and a little horseradish cream in each bowl for added flavor and spice.

PREPARE AHEAD The soup can be cooled, covered, and refrigerated for up to 2 days. Reheat before serving.

6 servings

prep 10 mins
• cook 45 mins

freeze for up to
3 months

Curried parsnip soup

The mix of sweet parsnips and gentle spices makes this soup a great winter warmer.

INGREDIENTS
3 tbsp butter
1 onion, chopped
11oz (300g) parsnips, chopped
1 carrot, chopped
1 baking potato, peeled and chopped
2 tbsp all-purpose flour
2 tbsp mild curry powder
4½ cups chicken or vegetable stock
salt and freshly ground black pepper
crème fraîche, for serving
chopped parsley, for serving

METHOD
1 Melt the butter in a saucepan over a medium heat. Add the onion and cook, stirring frequently, until softened. Add the parsnips, carrot, and potato. Sprinkle in the flour and curry powder and stir for 2 minutes.

2 Gradually stir in the stock. Turn up the heat and bring to a boil. Reduce the heat to low. Cover and simmer gently for 40 minutes, or until the vegetables are tender.

3 Turn the heat off, uncover, and allow the soup to cool slightly. Purée the soup in a blender or food processor. Season with salt and pepper. Pour back into the pot and reheat before serving.

4 To serve, ladle into bowls. Top each with a swirl of crème fraîche and a sprinkle of chopped parsley.

GOOD WITH Crusty bread or cheese scones.

4 servings

prep 10 mins
• cook 50 mins

36

French onion soup

This Parisian classic is given extra punch with a few spoonfuls of brandy.

INGREDIENTS

2 tbsp butter
1 tbsp vegetable oil
1½lb (675g) onions, thinly sliced
1 tsp sugar
salt and freshly ground pepper
½ cup dry red wine
2 tbsp all-purpose flour
6 cups hot beef stock
¼ cup brandy
1 garlic clove, cut in half
4 slices French baguette, about ¾in (2cm) thick, toasted
½ cup Gruyère or Emmenthal cheese, grated

METHOD

1 Melt the butter with the oil in a large, heavy saucepan over low heat. Stir in the onions and sugar, and season with salt and pepper. Press a piece of wax paper over the surface. Cook for 40 minutes, uncovering and stirring occasionally, until the onions are a rich, dark brown. Watch carefully to avoid scorching.

2 Remove the wax paper and stir in the wine. Increase the heat to medium and boil, stirring often, for 5 minutes, or until the wine reduces to a glaze. Sprinkle in the flour and cook, stirring often, for 2 minutes. Stir in the stock and bring to a boil. Reduce the heat to low, cover, and simmer for 30 minutes. Stir in the brandy and season to taste.

3 Meanwhile, place the broiler rack 8in (20cm) from the heat, and preheat the broiler. Divide the soup among the flame-proof bowls. Rub the garlic clove over the toast and place 1 slice in each bowl. Sprinkle with the cheese and broil for 2–3 minutes, or until the cheese is bubbling and golden. Serve at once.

PREPARE AHEAD Steps 1 and 2 can be completed up to a day ahead.

4 servings

**prep 10 mins
• cook 1 hr**

**4 flame-proof
soup bowls**

**the soup,
without bread
or cheese, can
be frozen for
up to 1 month**

Minestrone

This hearty soup makes a great lunch or dinner. Feel free to add whatever vegetables are in season.

INGREDIENTS

$\frac{1}{2}$ cup dried white cannellini (white kidney) beans
2 tbsp olive oil
2 celery stalks, finely chopped
2 carrots, finely chopped
1 onion, peeled and finely chopped
6 cups chicken stock or vegetable stock
one 14.5oz (400g) can chopped tomatoes
salt and freshly ground black pepper
$\frac{1}{2}$ cup elbow macaroni or ditalini
4 tbsp chopped parsley
$\frac{1}{2}$ cup freshly grated Parmesan cheese

METHOD

1 Put the beans in a large bowl, cover with cold water, and let soak overnight. Drain the beans and place in a large saucepan. Cover with fresh cold water and bring to a boil over high heat. Skim the surface as necessary. Boil for 10 minutes. Reduce the heat to low, partially cover the pan, and simmer for 1 hour or until just tender. Drain well and set aside.

2 In a large saucepan, heat the oil over medium heat. Add the celery, carrots, and onion, and cook, stirring occasionally, for 5 minutes or until tender. Stir in the beans, stock, tomatoes with their juice, and salt and pepper to taste. Bring to a boil, stirring occasionally. Reduce the heat, cover, and simmer for 20 minutes.

3 Add the pasta and simmer for 10–12 minutes longer, or until tender. Stir in the parsley and half the cheese. Season to taste. Pour into a warmed tureen, and sprinkle with the remaining Parmesan cheese. Serve hot.

GOOD WITH A dollop of pesto, stirred in before adding the cheese in step 3.

PREPARE AHEAD Steps 1 and 2 can be done up to a day ahead.

4–6 servings

prep 20 mins, plus soaking the beans • cook 1¾ hrs

soak the beans in advance

freeze for up to 1 month before the pasta is added in step 3

Winter vegetable soup

Some people call this "Penny Soup," because the vegetable pieces resemble coins.

INGREDIENTS

4 small red-skinned new potatoes
4 large carrots
1 medium sweet potato
1 leek, white and pale green parts only
1 tbsp butter
1 tbsp olive oil
2$\frac{1}{2}$ cups vegetable stock
salt and freshly ground black pepper

METHOD

1 Slice the potatoes, carrots, sweet potato, and leek crosswise into rounds about $\frac{1}{8}$ in (2–3mm) thick. The potatoes can be peeled or unpeeled. Rinse the leeks well.

2 Melt the butter with the oil in a large saucepan over medium-low heat. Add the leeks and cook, stirring occasionally, for 3–4 minutes, until beginning to soften. Add the potatoes, carrots, and sweet potato, and stir for 1 minute.

3 Pour in the stock, and bring to a boil over high heat. Reduce the heat to medium-low and simmer for 20 minutes, or until the vegetables are tender but not falling apart.

4 Transfer about one-third of the vegetables to a blender or food processor with the cooking liquid. Purée then return to the pan. Season with salt and pepper and serve hot.

PREPARE AHEAD The soup can be made 1 day ahead, cooled, covered, and refrigerated, or frozen for up to three months.

4 servings

prep 15 mins
• cook 25 mins

Tuna and pasta bake

Every cook should have a recipe for this quick one-dish meal, which is ideal at the end of a busy day.

INGREDIENTS
8oz (230g) pasta shells
one 10.75oz (305g) can condensed cream of mushroom soup
1 cup whole milk
one 6oz (170g) can tuna in water, drained and flaked
1 cup frozen corn, thawed
1 onion, finely chopped
1 small red bell pepper, cored, seeded, and finely chopped
3 tbsp chopped parsley
pinch of chili powder (optional)
1 cup shredded Cheddar cheese
salt and freshly ground black pepper

METHOD
1 Bring a large saucepan of salted water to a boil over high heat. Add the pasta, stir, and cook for 2 minutes less than the time on the package instructions.

2 Meanwhile, preheat the oven to 425°F (220°C). Butter an oven-proof casserole.

3 Drain the pasta. Bring the mushroom soup and milk to a simmer over low heat in the pasta pot. Add the tuna, corn, red pepper, parsley, chili powder, and half of the cheese, and mix. Stir in the cooked pasta. Season with salt and pepper.

4 Spread the mixture in the casserole. Sprinkle with the remaining cheese. Bake for about 30 minutes, or until the top is golden brown. Serve hot.

GOOD WITH Hot garlic bread and a green salad on the side.

PREPARE AHEAD The whole dish can be assembled, covered, and refrigerated several hours in advance. Remove the dish from the refrigerator at least 10 minutes before cooking.

4–6 servings

**prep 10 mins
• cook 40 mins**

Tofu and mushroom stroganoff

This recipe gives the traditional stroganoff a tasty vegetarian twist by substituting tofu chunks for the meat.

INGREDIENTS

2 tbsp vegetable oil
12oz (350g) firm tofu, cut into strips
1 red onion, thinly sliced
2 red bell peppers, seeded and sliced
9oz (250g) mixed mushrooms, quartered or sliced
2 garlic cloves, minced
$^2/_3$ cup vegetable stock
2 tbsp smooth peanut butter
2 tbsp tomato paste
2 tsp cornstarch
1 cup crème fraîche or sour cream
salt and freshly ground black pepper
2 tbsp finely chopped chives
boiled rice, to serve

METHOD

1 Heat 1 tbsp of the oil in a large frying pan or wok over medium-high heat. Stir-fry the tofu until golden. Transfer to a plate.

2 Add the remaining 1 tbsp oil to the pan and reduce the heat to medium. Add the onions, peppers, and mushrooms and cook, stirring often, about 5 minutes, or until softened. Stir in the garlic and cook 1 minute more.

3 Stir in the stock, peanut butter, and tomato paste. Return the tofu to the pan and bring to a simmer. Cook to blend the flavors, about 3 minutes. Dissolve the cornstarch in 2 tbsp cold water and stir into the simmering liquid. Cook about 1 minute, until thickened.

4 Stir in the crème fraîche and season with salt and pepper. Sprinkle with chives and serve hot with boiled rice.

4 servings

prep 15 mins
• cook 20 mins

Thai noodle stir-fry

A fragrant and colorful stir-fry with the flavors of Thailand.

INGREDIENTS

6oz (75g) cellophane (mung bean) noodles

3 tbsp peanut or vegetable oil

3 skinless and boneless chicken breasts,
    cut into thin strips

1 onion, sliced

4oz (115g) shiitake mushrooms, sliced

1 red bell pepper, seeded and sliced

1 lemongrass stalk, peeled and bottom part minced

1 tsp peeled and finely grated fresh ginger

1 fresh hot Thai red chili, seeded and minced

1 head of bok choy, shredded

2 tbsp soy sauce

1 tbsp Asian fish sauce

1 tsp sweet chili sauce

METHOD

1 Soak the noodles in a bowl of very hot water about 10 minutes, until softened. Drain well and rinse under cold running water. Cut into manageable lengths with kitchen scissors.

2 Heat 2 tbsp of the oil in a wok over high heat. Add the chicken and stir-fry about 3 minutes, or until lightly browned. Transfer to a plate.

3 Reduce the heat to medium and add the remaining 1 tbsp oil. Add the onion and stir-fry for 2 minutes. Add the mushrooms, bell pepper, lemongrass, ginger, and chili, and stir-fry about 2 minutes, or until the bell pepper softens.

4 Add the bok choy and stir-fry for about 2 minutes, or until wilted. Return the chicken to the pan and add the noodles. Pour in the soy sauce, fish sauce, and sweet chili sauce, and toss everything together over the heat for 2–3 minutes, or until piping hot. Serve hot.

4 servings

**prep 20 mins
• cook 15 mins**

low fat

Spaghetti with puttanesca

A spicy Sicilian pasta sauce that gets its edge from capers and olives.

INGREDIENTS
½ cup extra virgin olive oil
2 garlic cloves, finely chopped
½ fresh hot red chili, seeded and minced
1½lb (680g) ripe tomatoes,
    skinned, seeded, and chopped
1 cup pitted and chopped Kalamata olives
6 canned anchovy fillets,
    drained and finely chopped
3 tbsp capers, drained and rinsed
1lb (450g) spaghetti
2 tbsp chopped parsley

METHOD
1 Heat the oil in a medium saucepan over low heat. Add garlic and chili and cook, stirring often, for 2 minutes, or until the garlic is pale gold. Add the tomatoes, olives, anchovies, and capers and bring to a boil over high heat.

2 Return the heat to low and simmer, stirring frequently, for about 15 minutes, or until the juices thicken.

3 Cook the spaghetti in a pot of lightly salted boiling water over high heat according to the package instructions until *al dente*. Drain.

4 Toss the spaghetti with the sauce and sprinkle with the parsley. Serve hot.

GOOD WITH A glass of full-bodied red wine.

4–6 servings

prep 10 mins
• cook 10–15
mins

Pork and leek pie

A chunky pie with a crisp crust and a wholesome taste.

INGREDIENTS

2 tbsp vegetable oil
1lb (450g) boneless pork loin,
    cut into 1in (2.5cm) cubes
2 leeks, white and pale green parts,
    thickly sliced
6oz (175g) white mushrooms, halved
1 tsp chopped thyme
1 cup apple juice
$^2/_3$ cup chicken stock
2 tbsp tomato paste
salt and freshly ground black pepper
1 tbsp cornstarch
9oz (250g) ready-made pie crust pastry
1 large egg, beaten, to glaze

METHOD

1 Heat the oil in a frying pan. Brown the pork, remove, and set aside. Add the vegetables and thyme, and cook for 5 minutes. Add the apple juice, stock, tomato paste, and cornstarch and bring to a boil, stirring until thickened. Return the pork, season with salt and pepper, and simmer for 25 minutes; cool.

2 Transfer the pork and vegetables to a pie dish. Roll out the pastry and use to cover the dish, decorating the top with the trimmings. Make a hole in the pastry, glaze the pastry with the egg, and chill for 30 minutes. Preheat the oven to 400°F (200°C). Bake 35 minutes, until the pastry is browned.

GOOD WITH Steamed vegetables, such as broccoli and carrots.

4 servings

prep 25 mins,
plus cooling
• cook 1 hr
10 mins

Macaroni and three cheeses

This simple dish makes a nourishing family meal.

INGREDIENTS

1lb (450g) elbow macaroni
6 tbsp butter, plus more for the dish
1 cup fresh bread crumbs
$1/4$ cup all-purpose flour
1 tsp dry mustard
pinch of ground nutmeg
$1^3/_4$ cup whole milk, warmed
2 cups shredded sharp Cheddar cheese
4oz (115g) fresh mozzarella cheese,
    drained and finely diced
$1/2$ cup freshly grated Parmesan cheese

METHOD

1 Bring a large pot of lightly salted water to a boil over high heat. Add the macaroni and cook for 2 minutes less than the time on the package instructions. Drain well.

2 Meanwhile, preheat the oven to 400°F (200°C) and butter a 3qt (3 liter) oven-proof casserole. Melt 2 tbsp of the butter in a frying pan. Add the bread crumbs and stir to coat. Let cool.

3 Melt 4 tbsp butter in a large saucepan over medium heat. Whisk in the flour, and cook without browning for 30 seconds. Stir in the mustard and nutmeg. Remove the pan from the heat and slowly whisk in the milk. Return the pan to the heat and bring the mixture to the simmer, whisking almost constantly. Cook for 3 minutes. Remove from the heat. Stir in the Cheddar cheese until melted. Stir in the macaroni and mozzarella. Transfer to the baking dish and smooth the surface.

4 Stir the Parmesan cheese into the bread crumbs. Sprinkle over the macaroni and cheese. Place the dish on a baking sheet. Bake for 25 minutes, or until heated through and golden brown on top. Let stand for 2 minutes. Serve straight from the dish.

GOOD WITH A green salad or garlic bread.

PREPARE AHEAD The dish can be assembled up to a day in advance, covered, and refrigerated. Add the bread crumb and cheese topping just before baking.

6–8 servings

prep 20 mins
• cook 35 mins

Herb and goat cheese frittata

Thinner than a Spanish tortilla, this popular Italian dish is ideal for lunch or a light supper.

INGREDIENTS
6 large eggs
4 sage or basil leaves, finely chopped
salt and freshly ground black pepper
3 tbsp olive oil, plus extra for brushing
1 shallot, chopped
10 cherry tomatoes, halved
4oz (120g) rindless goat cheese, crumbled

METHOD
1 Preheat the broiler and position the rack 6in (15cm) from the heat. Beat the eggs in a bowl with the sage, season with salt and pepper, and set aside.

2 Heat the oil in the nonstick frying pan over medium-low heat. Add the shallot and cook, stirring constantly, for 3 minutes, or until just softened but not browned.

3 Add the eggs to the pan and stir gently to combine. Cover and cook gently for 2–3 minutes; the frittata should remain moist on top.

4 Arrange the tomatoes and goat cheese over the surface and lightly brush with olive oil. Place the pan in the broiler for 5 minutes or until the frittata is set and lightly browned. Let stand for 5 minutes. Slide onto a serving platter and cut into wedges. Serve hot, warm, or at room temperature.

GOOD WITH Plenty of Italian bread and a tomato salad.

4–6 servings

prep 10 mins
• cook 20 mins

9in (23cm)
nonstick frying
pan with a lid
and flame-proof
handle

HEARTY

Porcini mushroom soup

This hearty Italian country soup is full of deep, earthy goodness.

INGREDIENTS

1oz (30g) dried porcini mushrooms
1⅓ cups boiling water
3 tbsp extra virgin olive oil, plus more for drizzling
2 onions, finely chopped
2 celery stalks with leaves, finely chopped
4oz (115g) cremini mushrooms, sliced
2 garlic cloves, thinly sliced
2 tsp chopped rosemary
1 tsp chopped thyme
3 cups vegetable stock
one 14.5oz (411g) can chopped tomatoes, drained
salt and freshly ground black pepper
4 cups diced day-old crusty bread

METHOD

1 Combine the dried porcini and boiling water in a small bowl. Let stand for 30 minutes. Drain through a fine sieve, reserving the soaking liquid. Coarsely chop the soaked mushrooms.

2 Heat the oil in a large saucepan over medium-low heat. Add the onions and cook about 5 minutes, until softened. Add the celery and cook 5 minutes more, until the celery is tender. Stir in the mushrooms, garlic, rosemary, and thyme and cook until the mushrooms soften, about 5 minutes more.

3 Add the stock, tomatoes, and the soaked mushrooms and their liquid. Bring to a boil over high heat. Return the heat to medium-low and simmer for 45 minutes.

4 Stir in the bread. Season with salt and pepper. Remove from the heat, cover, and let stand for 10 minutes. Stir well so the bread can break up and thicken the soup. Spoon into deep bowls, drizzle each serving with olive oil, and serve hot.

GOOD WITH Bowls of spiced olives, and crusty bread.

PREPARE AHEAD The soup can be made through step 3, then cooled, covered, and refrigerated for up to 2 days. Reheat, then add the bread.

6 servings

prep 20 mins,
• cook 1 hr,
plus standing

low fat, low GI

freeze, without
the bread, for
up to 3 months

Tuscan bean soup

This soup, *ribollita*, is thick, filling, nutritious, and delicious. It is even wonderful at room temperature.

INGREDIENTS

¼ cup extra virgin olive oil, plus more for serving
1 onion, chopped
2 carrots, sliced
1 leek, white and pale green parts only, sliced
2 garlic cloves, chopped
1 quart (1 liter) chicken stock
one 14.5oz (411g) can chopped tomatoes
1 tbsp tomato paste
one 15oz (420g) can white kidney (cannellini) beans,
    drained and rinsed
9oz (250g) spinach, sliced
salt and freshly ground black pepper
8 slices Italian bread
2 tbsp grated Parmesan (optional), for serving

METHOD

1 Heat the oil in a soup pot over medium-low heat. Add the onion, carrots, and leek and cook until softened but not colored. Add the garlic and cook for 1 minute. Add the stock, tomatoes and their juices, and tomato paste.

2 In a bowl, mash half the beans with a fork and stir into the pot. Bring to a boil over high heat. Return the heat to medium-low and simmer for 30 minutes.

3 Add the remaining beans and spinach and simmer for 30 minutes more.

4 Place a slice of bread in each soup bowl. Ladle in the soup, and, if you like, top with a sprinkling of Parmesan.

GOOD WITH A dollop of pesto placed on top and olive oil passed on the side.

PREPARE AHEAD This soup is best made ahead and reheated.

8 servings

prep 15 mins
• cook 1 hr
20 mins

New England clam chowder

Serve this rich, creamy soup with plenty of saltines or crusty bread.

INGREDIENTS
36 littleneck clams
1 tbsp oil
4 strips bacon, sliced
1 onion, finely chopped
2 baking potatoes, such as russet,
   peeled and cut into $\frac{1}{2}$in (1cm) cubes
2 tbsp all-purpose flour
$2\frac{1}{2}$ cups whole milk
salt and freshly ground black pepper
$\frac{1}{2}$ cup heavy cream
2 tbsp finely chopped parsley

METHOD
1 Place the clams and $\frac{1}{4}$ cup water in a large saucepan. Cover and cook over high heat, shaking the pan, until the clams open. Using tongs, transfer the clams to a bowl. Strain the liquid through a wire sieve lined with paper towels to remove grit. Add enough water to measure 2 cups. Remove the clams from the shells. Coarsely chop the clams, cover, and chill.

2 Heat the oil in a large, heavy pan over medium heat. Add the bacon and cook until crispy. Using a slotted spoon, transfer to paper towels to drain.

3 Add the onion and potatoes to the pan. Cook for 5 minutes, or until the onion has softened. Stir in the flour and cook for 2 minutes.

4 Stir in the clam juice and milk and season with salt and pepper. Cover, reduce the heat, and simmer for 20 minutes or until the potatoes are tender. Stir in the cream and clams, and heat through without boiling. Season and serve hot, topped with the bacon and parsley.

PREPARE AHEAD Steps 1 and 2 can be completed several hours in advance; keep the clams refrigerated until ready to use.

4–6 servings

prep 15 mins
• cook 35 mins

**cook clams
on day of
purchase**

Spanish stew

A filling one-pot meal known as *Cocido* in Spain.

INGREDIENTS
4 tbsp olive oil
4 small onions, quartered
2 garlic cloves, sliced
9oz (250g) beef chuck, cut into 4 thick slices
6oz (175g) slab bacon, cut into 4 thick pieces
4 pork spareribs, cut into ribs
4 thick slices pork belly, about 18oz (500g) in total
4 chicken thighs
1½ cups white wine
6oz (175g) smoked chorizo, cut into 4 pieces
6oz (175g) morcilla (Spanish blood sausage)
1 smoked ham hock
1 bay leaf
salt and freshly ground black pepper
8 small boiling potatoes
4 carrots, halved lengthwise
1 head Savoy cabbage, quartered
one 15oz (420g) can chickpeas
3 tbsp chopped parsley, to garnish

METHOD
1 Heat 1 tbsp oil in a saucepan over medium-low heat. Add the onions and garlic and cook, stirring, for 10 minutes, until softened.

2 Heat the remaining 3 tbsp oil in a frying pan over medium-high heat. In batches, brown the meats and chicken. Add to the saucepan with the onions and garlic.

3 Pour the wine into the frying pan and boil over high heat, scraping up the bits, for 3 minutes, or until reduced by half. Pour into the saucepan. Add the chorizo, morcilla, ham hock, and bay leaf. Add cold water to cover and season. Bring to a boil. Cover, reduce the heat, and simmer for 1½ hours.

4 Add the potatoes and carrots and simmer for 30 minutes. Add the cabbage and garbanzo beans and cook until the meats are very tender, about 15 minutes more. Discard the bay leaf and ham hock. Divide the meat and vegetables among 4 bowls. Ladle in some of the broth, sprinkle with the parsley, and serve hot.

GOOD WITH Roast potatoes, and vegetables of your choice.

4 servings

**prep 25 mins
• cook 2 hrs
45 mins**

Pappardelle with ragù

This meaty, slow-simmered sauce goes well with pasta ribbons, but is also delicious served with tagliatelle or used in lasagna.

INGREDIENTS

2 tbsp butter
2 tbsp olive oil
4oz (125g) pancetta, diced
1 small onion, finely chopped
1 celery stalk, finely chopped
1 carrot, finely chopped
2 garlic cloves, minced
1lb (450g) ground round
one 14.5oz (411g) can chopped tomatoes
$\frac{1}{2}$ cup beef stock, as needed
2 tbsp tomato paste
salt and freshly ground black pepper
$\frac{1}{3}$ cup whole milk, heated
1lb (450g) dried pappardelle
freshly grated Parmesan, to serve

METHOD

1 Melt the butter and the oil in a large saucepan over medium heat. Add the pancetta and cook for 2 minutes, until it gives off some fat. Add the onion, celery, carrot, and garlic and cook, stirring, 10 minutes, or until softened but not browned.

2 Stir in the ground round and cook for 10 minutes, stirring and breaking it up with a spoon, until browned. Stir in the canned tomatoes, stock, and tomato paste, and season. Bring to a boil.

3 Reduce the heat and partially cover the saucepan. Simmer, stirring occasionally and adding more stock, if needed, for $1\frac{1}{2}$ hours. Stir in the milk and simmer for 30 minutes more, until thick and well flavored.

4 Bring a saucepan of lightly salted water to a boil, add the pappardelle, and cook until *al dente*. Drain well. Transfer to a serving bowl and add the ragù. Toss and serve hot, with the Parmesan.

4 servings

prep 15 mins • cook 2 hrs

freeze the sauce for up to 3 months

Macaroni bake with ham and peppers

Quick to make and full of rich flavors, this pasta casserole makes a satisfying midweek meal or an informal dinner party dish.

INGREDIENTS

1lb (450g) elbow macaroni or other tube-shaped pasta
1 tbsp olive oil
1 red onion, thinly sliced
1 garlic clove, crushed
1 red bell pepper, seeded and thinly sliced
one 14.5oz (411g) can chopped tomatoes
9oz (250g) smoked ham, diced
3 tbsp dry white wine or chicken stock
2 tsp dried oregano
salt and freshly ground black pepper
1 cup fresh bread crumbs
3 tbsp freshly grated Parmesan
2 tbsp butter, melted

METHOD

1 Preheat the oven to 400°F (200°C). Bring a large saucepan of salted water to a boil. Add the macaroni and cook according to the package instructions, until barely tender. Drain well.

2 Meanwhile, heat the oil in a saucepan over medium heat. Add the onion, garlic, and red pepper, and cook, stirring occasionally, for about 5 minutes, or until softened but not browned.

3 Add the tomatoes, ham, wine, and oregano and bring to a boil. Simmer for 2–3 minutes to reduce slightly. Remove from the heat. Stir in the macaroni and season with salt and pepper. Spread in a 2 quart (2 liter) baking dish. Mix the bread crumbs, Parmesan, and butter, and sprinkle on top.

4 Place on a baking sheet and bake for 15–20 minutes, or until golden and bubbling. Serve hot.

GOOD WITH A spinach salad.

PREPARE AHEAD Prepare through step 3; cool, cover with aluminum foil, and refrigerate for up to 1 day. Bake 15 minutes, remove the foil and bake 15 minutes more, until well heated.

6–8 servings

prep 10 mins • cook 20–25 mins

Pad Thai

Once you have gathered the ingredients, this dish comes together quickly to create a fast weeknight supper.

INGREDIENTS

12oz (350g) flat rice noodles
4 tbsp vegetable oil
2 tbsp chopped cilantro
1 small hot red chili, seeded and finely chopped
9oz (250g) large shrimp, peeled and deveined
4 shallots, finely chopped
4 large eggs, beaten
1 tbsp sugar
2 tbsp oyster sauce
1 tbsp Thai fish sauce
2 tbsp fresh lime juice
9oz (250g) bean sprouts
4 scallions, white and green parts, sliced
1 cup unsalted roasted peanuts
1 lime cut into 4 wedges, to serve

METHOD

1 Soak the noodles in a bowl of hot water to cover for about 15 minutes, or until soft. Drain.

2 Meanwhile, heat a wok or large frying pan over high heat. Add 2 tbsp of the oil, then the cilantro and chili. Immediately add the shrimp and stir-fry until the shrimp look opaque around the edges, about 1 minute. Transfer to a plate.

3 Add the remaining oil to the wok. Add the shallots and stir-fry for 1 minute. Add the eggs and sugar and cook, stirring, for 1 minute, until the eggs are scrambled.

4 Stir in the oyster sauce, fish sauce, and lime juice. Add the noodles, bean sprouts, and shrimp. Stir-fry for 2 minutes. Add the scallions and $1/2$ cup of the peanuts, and stir-fry for 1 minute. Sprinkle with the remaining peanuts and garnish with lime wedges to serve.

GOOD WITH A fresh salad of bean sprouts and shredded carrot, tossed with lime juice.

4 servings

prep 20 mins
• cook 10 mins

Vegetable curry

In Indian cooking, cardamom, cloves, coriander, and cumin seeds are all considered "warming spices" that heat the body from within, making this an excellent winter dish.

INGREDIENTS

1/4 cup vegetable oil

10oz (300g) red-skinned potatoes, diced

5 green cardamom pods, crushed

3 whole cloves

1 cinnamon stick, broken in half

2 tsp cumin seeds

1 onion, finely chopped

2 tsp peeled and grated fresh ginger

2 large garlic cloves, crushed

1 1/2 tsp ground turmeric

1 tsp ground coriander

salt and freshly ground black pepper

one 14.5oz (411g) can chopped tomatoes

pinch of sugar

2 carrots, diced

2 fresh hot green chilies,
   seeded (optional) and sliced into thin rounds

1 cup sliced Savoy or green cabbage

1 cup cauliflower florets

1 cup thawed frozen peas

2 tbsp chopped cilantro

toasted sliced almonds, to garnish

METHOD

1 Heat the oil in a large frying pan over high heat. Add the potatoes and cook, stirring often, for 5 minutes, or until golden brown. Using a slotted spoon, transfer to paper towels to drain.

2 Reduce the heat to medium. Add the cardamom pods, cloves, cinnamon, and cumin seeds and stir until the spices are very fragrant. Add the onion and cook, stirring often, for about 5 minutes, or until softened. Add the ginger, garlic, turmeric, and coriander, and season with salt and pepper. Stir for 1 minute.

3 Stir in the tomatoes with their juices and the sugar. Return the potatoes to the pan, add the carrots, chilies, and 1 cup of water, and bring to a boil, stirring often. Reduce the heat to low. Simmer, stirring occasionally, for 15 minutes, or until the carrots are just tender, adding a little water if needed.

4 Stir in the cabbage, cauliflower, and peas. Return the heat to medium and simmer for about 10 minutes, or until the vegetables are tender. Stir in the cilantro and season again. Remove and discard the cardamom pods and cloves. Transfer to a serving bowl, sprinkle with almonds, and serve hot.

GOOD WITH Lots of basmati rice or naan bread.

PREPARE AHEAD The curry can be made 1 day ahead, covered and refrigerated. Reheat over low heat, adding water if the sauce is too thick.

4–6 servings

prep 20 mins
• cook 35–45 mins

freeze for up to
3 months

Kedgeree

This Anglo-Indian brunch dish is traditionally made with smoked haddock, but you can use all fresh salmon if you wish.

INGREDIENTS
10oz (280g) smoked haddock (Finnan haddie)
10oz (280g) fresh salmon fillets
1 cup basmati rice
$\frac{1}{8}$ tsp crumbled saffron
salt and freshly ground pepper
4 tbsp butter
4 hard-boiled eggs
2 tbsp chopped parsley, plus more for garnish
1 lemon, cut into wedges

METHOD
1 Place the haddock in a single layer in a large frying pan. Add enough water to cover and heat over medium heat until just simmering. Reduce the heat to low, and simmer for 7 minutes. Using a slotted spoon, transfer the fish to a plate and cool.

2 Meanwhile, bring the rice, 2 cups water, saffron, and $\frac{1}{2}$ tsp salt to a boil in a medium saucepan. Reduce the heat to low and cover. Simmer about 15 minutes, until the rice is tender. Remove from heat and stir in the butter.

3 Remove the yolks from the hard-boiled eggs; chop finely, and set aside. Chop the egg whites and stir into the rice with the flaked fish and 2 tbsp chopped parsley.

4 Spoon onto heated plates, sprinkle with the chopped egg yolk and parsley, and serve with the lemon wedge.

GOOD WITH Triangles of buttered whole wheat toast.

4 servings

prep 20 mins
• cook 20 mins

Vegetable biryani

A satisfying dish that both vegetarians and meat-eaters will enjoy.

INGREDIENTS

1³/₄ cups basmati rice
1 large carrot, sliced
2 boiling potatoes, peeled and cut into small dice
¹/₂ cauliflower, cut into small florets
3 tbsp vegetable oil
1 red onion, chopped
1 red bell pepper, seeded and chopped
1 green bell pepper, seeded and chopped
1 zucchini, chopped
²/₃ cup frozen peas
2 tsp ground coriander
2 tsp curry powder
1 tsp ground turmeric
1 tsp chili powder
1 tsp cumin seeds
²/₃ cup vegetable stock
¹/₂ cup cashew nuts, lightly toasted

METHOD

1 Bring a large saucepan of water to a boil over high heat. Add the rice and cook until just tender, about 15 minutes. Drain well.

2 Cook the carrot and potatoes in another saucepan of salted boiling water until half done, about 5 minutes. Add the cauliflower and cook about 5 minutes more, until all of the vegetables are tender. Drain.

3 Heat the oil in a large frying pan over medium heat. Add the onion and cook, stirring often, about 5 minutes, or until softened. Add the red and green peppers and the zucchini and cook, stirring often, until crisp and tender, about 5 minutes.

4 Stir the reserved vegetables and peas into the frying pan. Add the coriander, curry powder, turmeric, chili powder, and cumin. Cook for 1 minute, stirring often, until the spices are fragrant.

5 Meanwhile, preheat the oven to 350°F (180°C). Spread half the rice into a baking dish, top with the vegetable mixture, and then the remaining rice. Cover with aluminum foil. Bake for 30 minutes, or until hot. Sprinkle with cashews and serve.

GOOD WITH Naan bread, mango chutney, lime pickle, or raita.

4 servings

prep 30 mins
• cook 45 mins

low fat

Sweet and sour shrimp

This is a fresher, lighter version of the Chinese take-out standard, with a fragrant sauce spiked with chili, garlic, and ginger.

INGREDIENTS

3 tbsp rice wine vinegar
2 tbsp honey
2 tbsp soy sauce
2 tbsp ketchup
1 tbsp sugar
2 tbsp vegetable oil
1 green bell pepper, seeded and cut into strips
1 small carrot, cut into matchsticks
1 celery stalk, cut into matchsticks
3 shallots, peeled and sliced
1 tbsp peeled and grated fresh ginger
1 fresh hot red chili, seeded and minced
1 garlic clove, minced
1lb (450g) medium shrimp, peeled and deveined
2 scallions, white and green parts, cut into thin strips

METHOD

1 Stir the vinegar, honey, soy sauce, sugar, and ketchup in a small pan over a low heat until the sugar is melted.

2 Heat the oil in a large frying pan or wok over high heat. Add the green pepper, carrot, celery, shallots, ginger, chili, and garlic. Stir-fry until the green pepper softens, about 3 minutes.

3 Add the shrimp and stir-fry for about 2 minutes or until they turn pink. Pour in the vinegar mixture and stir-fry for 1 minute until the shrimp and vegetables are coated and everything is heated through.

4 Transfer to a platter and garnish with the scallions. Serve hot.

GOOD WITH Hot cooked rice.

4 servings

prep 20 mins
• cook 10 mins

wok

Shrimp diablo

If hot as the "devil," is too hot, use less of the hot red pepper.

INGREDIENTS

2 tbsp olive oil
1 onion, chopped
1 red bell pepper, seeded and sliced
3 garlic cloves, minced
$\frac{1}{2}$ cup dry white wine
1 cup canned crushed tomatoes
$\frac{1}{2}$ tsp crushed hot red pepper, or more to taste
1lb (450g) large shrimp, peeled and deveined
2 tsp Worcestershire sauce

METHOD

1 Heat the oil in a large frying pan over medium heat. Add the onion and cook about 5 minutes, until beginning to turn golden. Add the red pepper and cook for 5 minutes more, until softened.

2 Stir in the garlic and cook for 1 minute, or until fragrant. Stir in the wine and boil about 2 minutes until reduced by half.

3 Stir in the tomatoes and bring to a boil. Reduce the heat to medium-low and simmer about 5 minutes, or until slightly reduced. Season with crushed hot pepper.

4 Stir in the shrimp and cook about 3 minutes, or until they turn opaque. Stir in Worcestershire sauce and serve immediately.

GOOD WITH Steamed rice.

PREPARE AHEAD The sauce can be prepared up to 2 hours ahead; add the shrimp just before serving.

4 servings

**prep 5 mins
• cook 20 mins**

Shellfish and tomato stew

This rustic stew is delicious served for lunch or dinner.

INGREDIENTS
2 tbsp olive oil
2 shallots, finely chopped
1 celery stalk, finely chopped
2 garlic cloves, chopped
2 anchovies in oil, rinsed and chopped
pinch of crushed hot red pepper
salt and freshly ground black pepper
one 14.5oz (411g) can chopped tomatoes
1 cup dry white wine
1 cup bottled clam juice
8oz (230g) large shrimp, peeled and deveined
8oz (230g) sea scallops
3 tbsp fresh lemon juice
1 tsp capers, drained and rinsed

METHOD
1 Heat the oil over medium heat. Add the shallots, celery, garlic, anchovies, and hot pepper. Cook, stirring often, until softened. Stir in the tomatoes, wine, and clam juice, bring to a boil, then simmer for 20 minutes.

2 Add the shrimp, scallops, lemon juice, and capers. Cook about 5 minutes, or until the seafood is opaque. Season with salt and pepper.

GOOD WITH Toasted ciabatta.

4 servings

prep 10 mins
• cook 30 mins

Cod in tomato sauce

The tomatoes and wine add sweetness to this Spanish dish.

INGREDIENTS

2 tbsp olive oil

2¼lb (1kg) cod fillet, cut into 4 portions

1 large onion, finely sliced

1 garlic clove, minced

1¼ cups fish stock

4 large ripe plum tomatoes,
    peeled, seeded, and chopped

½ cup white wine

2 tsp tomato paste

½ tsp sugar

2 tbsp chopped parsley

salt and freshly ground black pepper

METHOD

1 Preheat the oven to 400°F (200°C). Heat the oil in the casserole over medium-high heat. Add the fish, skin side down, and cook, for 1 minute, or until the skin is crisp. Turn and cook for 1 minute longer. Using a slotted spatula, transfer to a plate.

2 Add the onions and garlic to the casserole and reduce the heat to medium. Cook, stirring frequently, for about 4 minutes, until softened. Add the stock, tomatoes, wine, and tomato paste and bring to a simmer. Simmer, stirring often, for 10–12 minutes.

3 Place the fish in the sauce and bake for 5–10 minutes, or until barely opaque. Transfer the fish to a platter and tent with aluminum foil to keep warm.

4 Cook the sauce over medium-high heat about 3 minutes, until reduced and thickened. Stir in half the parsley and season to taste with salt and pepper. Divide the sauce among 4 dinner plates and place a piece of fish on top. Serve at once, sprinkled with the remaining parsley.

4 servings

**prep 10 mins
• cook 30 mins**

**large
flame-proof
casserole**

Chicken paprikash

Spicy paprika adds both flavor and color to this hearty stew from Hungary.

INGREDIENTS

2 tbsp vegetable oil
8 chicken thighs
2 small red onions, sliced
1 garlic clove, finely chopped
1 tbsp sweet paprika
$\frac{1}{4}$ tsp caraway seeds
1 cup hot chicken stock
1 tbsp red wine vinegar
1 tbsp tomato paste
1 tsp sugar
salt and freshly ground black pepper
9oz (250g) cherry tomatoes
chopped parsley, to garnish
sour cream, to serve

METHOD

1 Heat the oil in the casserole over medium-high heat. Add the chicken thighs, skin side down. Cook about 3 minutes until the skin is golden. Turn and brown the other sides, about 2 minutes. Transfer to a plate.

2 Add the onions to the fat in the pan and cook, stirring often, for about 5 minutes, or until the onions are softened. Add the garlic and cook about 1 minute, until fragrant. Add the paprika and caraway seeds and stir for 1 minute. Return the chicken to the pan.

3 Mix together the stock, vinegar, tomato paste, sugar, and salt and pepper to taste. Pour over the chicken. Bring to a boil, then reduce the heat to low. Cover and simmer for 35 minutes, or until the chicken is tender.

4 Add the cherry tomatoes to the casserole and shake vigorously to mix them into the sauce. Cover and simmer for 5 minutes. Sprinkle with parsley and serve hot with sour cream on the side for each diner to help themselves.

GOOD WITH Creamy mashed potatoes or buttered noodles.

PREPARE AHEAD Steps 1–3 can be prepared up to 2 days in advance. Reheat with the tomatoes, ensuring the chicken is heated through.

4 servings

prep 10 mins
• cook 40–45 mins

large flame-proof casserole

can be frozen, without parsley or sour cream, for up to 1 month; thaw before cooking

Creamy tarragon chicken

Fresh tarragon and cream is a classic pairing in French cuisine.

INGREDIENTS

2 tbsp butter
1 tbsp canola oil
4 chicken breasts, with skin and bones
9oz (250g) shallots, sliced
1 tsp dried *herbes de Provence*
2 garlic cloves, finely chopped
salt and freshly ground black pepper
1 cup hot chicken stock
½ cup dry white wine
1 cup crème fraîche
2 tbsp chopped tarragon,
    plus extra sprigs to garnish

METHOD

1 Melt the butter with the oil in the casserole over medium-high heat. Add the chicken breasts, skin sides down, and cook for 3 minutes, or until golden brown. Turn them over and brown the other sides, about 2 minutes more.

2 Turn the chicken breasts skin sides up, then sprinkle with the shallots, *herbes de Provence*, garlic, and salt and pepper to taste. Add the stock and wine and bring to a boil. Reduce the heat to low, cover the casserole, and simmer for 25 minutes, or until the chicken is tender and the juices run clear when pierced with the tip of a knife. Transfer the chicken to a platter and tent with aluminum foil. Boil the sauce over high heat until reduced by about half.

3 Stir in the crème fraîche and chopped tarragon and continue boiling until thickened. If the sauce becomes too thick, add more chicken stock; then adjust the seasoning, if necessary. Coat the chicken with the sauce, garnish with the tarragon, and serve hot.

GOOD WITH Boiled long-grain rice, or try mashed potatoes with olive oil, and chopped pitted black olives.

PREPARE AHEAD Steps 1 and 2 can be prepared up to 1 day in advance and kept in a covered container in the refrigerator. Reheat and make sure the chicken is completely heated through before stirring in the crème fraîche.

4 servings

**prep 10 mins
• cook 35 mins**

large flame-proof casserole

the dish can be left to cool completely after step 2, then frozen for up to 1 month; thaw at room temperature, then complete the recipe

Chicken stew with herb dumplings

This hearty winter casserole is a main meal in itself, but is especially good when served with freshly steamed vegetables.

INGREDIENTS
4 chicken thighs
4 chicken drumsticks
salt and freshly ground black pepper
$1/3$ cup all-purpose flour
3 tbsp olive oil
2 carrots, sliced
2 leeks, cleaned and sliced
2 celery stalks, sliced
$1/2$ rutabaga, pared and diced
2 cups chicken stock
2 tbsp Worcestershire sauce

For the dumplings
1 cup all-purpose flour
1 tsp baking powder
1 tsp dried Italian seasoning
$1/4$ tsp salt
$1/8$ tsp freshly ground black pepper
4 tbsp butter, cut into small cubes
1 tbsp chopped parsley
$1/3$ cup milk, as needed

4 servings

**prep 15 mins
• cook 50 mins**

**large flame-
proof casserole**

**freeze, without
dumplings, for
up to 3 months**

METHOD

1 Season the chicken with salt and pepper. Dredge in the flour to coat. Heat 2 tbsp oil in the casserole over medium-high heat. In batches, add the chicken, turning occasionally, until golden brown. Transfer to a plate. Pour the fat from the pan.

2 Add the remaining oil to the pan. Add the carrots, leeks, celery, and rutabaga and cook, stirring occasionally, until beginning to brown. Stir in the stock and Worcestershire sauce. Return the chicken to the pan and simmer, covered, for 20 minutes.

3 Meanwhile, whisk the flour, baking powder, dried herbs, salt, and pepper in a medium bowl. Cut in the butter until the mixture resembles coarse bread crumbs. Add the parsley and stir in enough milk to make a soft dough. Divide into 12 balls.

4 Arrange 12 spoonfuls of the dough in the stew, cover, and simmer for 20 minutes. Serve hot.

Pot roast of guinea hen with cabbage and walnuts

Guinea hens gently simmered in broth are moist and flavorful, with all of the tasty juices sealed in the pot.

INGREDIENTS

2 guinea hens, about 2¾lb (1.25kg) each
salt and freshly ground black pepper
2 tbsp butter
2 tbsp olive oil
4 strips bacon, diced
1 small onion, finely chopped
1 leek, white and pale green part only,
   cleaned and thinly sliced
2 celery stalks, sliced
¾ cup walnut halves
1 small Savoy cabbage, about 14oz (400g),
   cut into 8 wedges
½ cup hot chicken stock

METHOD

1 Preheat the oven to 400°F (200°C). Season the hens inside and out with salt and pepper.

2 Heat the butter with 1 tbsp of the oil in the casserole over medium heat. Add the hens and cook, turning occasionally, for about 10 minutes, until browned. Transfer the hens to a platter.

3 Add the remaining oil to the casserole. Add the bacon, onion, leek, and celery and cook, stirring often, for about 3 minutes, until lightly colored. Add the walnuts. Return the hens to the casserole.

4 Tuck the cabbage wedges loosely into the pot and season with salt and pepper. Pour in the hot stock. Bring to a boil and cover. Bake for 40–45 minutes, or until the vegetables are tender and the guinea hen juices run clear with no sign of pink when pierced with the tip of a sharp knife.

5 Remove from the oven and let stand for 10 minutes. Transfer the hens to a carving board and cut each in half or into quarters. Place on dinner plates, top with the vegetables and pan juices, and serve hot.

4 servings

**prep 20 mins
• cook 40–45 mins**

**large, deep
flame-proof
casserole**

Hoppin' John

This is a traditional dish from the South.

INGREDIENTS

2 smoked ham hocks, about $2\frac{1}{4}$lb (1.1kg)
1 fresh bouquet garni, with 1 celery rib,
   4 thyme sprigs, and 1 bay leaf
   tied together with kitchen twine
2 large onions, chopped
$\frac{1}{4}$ tsp crushed hot red pepper
1 tbsp vegetable oil
1 cup long-grain rice
2 cans (15.5oz/440g) black-eyed peas,
   drained and rinsed
hot pepper sauce, to serve

METHOD

1 Put the ham hock in a large saucepan and add enough cold water to cover. Slowly bring to a boil over high heat, skimming the surface as necessary. Reduce the heat to low, add the bouquet garni, half the onions, and the hot pepper. Re-cover the pan again and simmer for $2\frac{1}{2}$ hours, or until the meat is very tender when pierced with the tip of a knife.

2 Place a colander over a large heat-proof bowl and strain the cooking liquid. Reserve the liquid and set the ham hock aside to cool.

3 Meanwhile, heat the oil in the casserole over a medium heat. Add the remaining onions and cook for 5 minutes until softened but not browned, stirring occasionally. Stir in the rice.

4 Stir in 2 cups of the reserved cooking liquid, the beans, and salt and pepper to taste. Bring to a boil, reduce the heat to low, cover tightly, and simmer for 20 minutes.

5 Meanwhile, remove the meat from the ham hock and cut into chunks; discard skin and bones.

6 Remove the casserole from the heat and let stand for 5 minutes, covered. Use a fork to stir in the ham. Pile the mixture onto a large serving platter and serve with hot pepper sauce on the side.

PREPARE AHEAD Step 1 can be prepared 1 day in advance. Chill the meat until ready to use.

4–6 servings

prep 12 mins
• cook 3–3½ hrs

flame-proof
casserole with
fitted lid

Chili con carne

This Tex-Mex classic makes a colorful family supper. Serve it with bowls of other flavorful dishes so everyone can help themselves.

INGREDIENTS

1 tbsp olive oil
1 onion, thinly sliced
1 garlic clove, crushed
2 tbsp chili powder
1 tsp ground cumin
1½lb (675g) ground round
one 15oz (420g) can red kidney beans,
    drained and rinsed
one 14.5oz (411g) can chopped tomatoes
2 tbsp tomato paste
salt and freshly ground black pepper
chopped cilantro and sour cream

METHOD

1 Heat the oil in a large saucepan over medium heat. Add the onions and cook for 5 minutes, or until softened. Add the garlic and cook 1 minute. Stir in the chili powder and cumin, then the beef. Cook, breaking up the beef with a spoon, until it browns all over, about 5 minutes.

2 Stir in the beans, tomatoes, and tomato paste and bring to a boil. Reduce the heat, cover, and simmer for 40 minutes, stirring occasionally, until thickened. Season with salt and pepper. Serve hot, sprinkled with cilantro and topped with sour cream.

GOOD WITH Rice or nachos, and bowls of guacamole and salsa.

4–6 servings

prep 5 mins
• cook 50 mins

freeze for up to
3 months

Roast lamb with white beans

French cooks prefer delicate flageolet beans for this rustic dish, but any small white bean will do.

INGREDIENTS

3lb (1.35kg) leg of lamb, or shanks
2–3 sprigs rosemary
1 tbsp olive oil
salt and freshly ground black pepper
two 15oz (440g) cans flageolet or white Northern beans, drained
4 plum tomatoes, cut in halves lengthwise
4 garlic cloves, coarsely chopped
²/₃ cup dry white wine
1 tbsp tomato paste

METHOD

1 Preheat the oven to 350°F (180°C). With a small, sharp knife, make several deep cuts into the flesh of the lamb. Strip the leaves from 1 rosemary sprig, and push a few rosemary leaves into each cut. Place the lamb in a roasting pan with the oil, and season with salt and pepper.

2 Bake for 1 hour. Combine the beans, tomatoes, garlic, and remaining rosemary. Remove the lamb from the oven and spoon the bean mixture around it. Mix the wine and tomato paste together and pour over the beans.

3 Cover the pan with aluminum foil, then continue baking for about 30 minutes, stirring the beans after 15 minutes, until a thermometer inserted in the thickest part of the lamb reads 130°F. Let stand for 15 minutes before serving.

PREPARE AHEAD The lamb can be prepared through step 1 and refrigerated up to 1 day.

4 servings

**prep 15 mins
• cook 1hr 30
mins**

Lamb tagine with couscous

Dried apricots and orange juice, along with cumin, coriander, ginger, and thyme, give this the distinct flavor and aroma of Moroccan cuisine.

INGREDIENTS

1 onion, thinly sliced
1 tsp ground cumin
1 tsp ground coriander
1 tsp ground ginger
1 tsp dried thyme
2 tbsp vegetable oil
2lb (900g) boneless lamb, such as shoulder,
　cut into 1in (2.5cm) cubes
2 tbsp all-purpose flour
1½ cups fresh orange juice
2 cups chicken stock
salt and freshly ground black pepper
4oz (120g) dried apricots
mint leaves, to garnish

For the couscous

1 cup plus 2 tbsp quick-cook couscous
salt

METHOD

1 Put the onion, cumin, coriander, ginger, thyme, and 1 tbsp of the oil in a large, nonmetallic bowl. Add the lamb and stir well. Cover and refrigerate for at least 3 hours or overnight.

2 When ready to cook, preheat the oven to 325°F (160°C). Put the flour in a small bowl and slowly whisk in the orange juice until smooth, then set aside.

3 Heat the remaining oil in the casserole over a high heat. Add the spiced lamb and cook, stirring frequently, for about 5 minutes, or until browned.

4 Stir the orange juice mixture into the casserole with the stock. Season with salt and pepper. Bring to a boil, stirring often. Cover and bake for 1 hour.

5 Remove the casserole from the oven. Stir in the apricots. Return to the oven and bake for 20 minutes more, or until the lamb is tender.

6 Meanwhile, prepare the couscous. Mix the couscous with salt to taste in a large heat-proof bowl and add boiling water to cover by 1in (2.5cm). Cover with a folded dish towel and let stand for 10 minutes, or until the couscous is tender. Fluff with a fork and keep warm. When the lamb is tender, taste and adjust the seasoning. Sprinkle with mint leaves and serve with the hot couscous.

PREPARE AHEAD The tagine can be cooked up to 2 days in advance.

4 servings

prep 10 mins, plus at least 3 hrs marinating • cook 1½ hrs

large flame-proof casserole

can be frozen for up to 1 month; thaw over low heat, then bring to a boil

Braised lamb

This dish packs plenty of flavor with its tomato, olive, and herb sauce.

INGREDIENTS
2lbs (900g) lamb leg steaks
salt and freshly ground black pepper
$\frac{1}{4}$ cup olive oil
1 large onion, peeled
2 garlic cloves, peeled
1 fresh hot red chili or $\frac{1}{2}$ tsp hot red pepper flakes
$\frac{1}{4}$ cup hearty red wine
one 14.5oz (411g) can chopped tomatoes
$\frac{2}{3}$ cup pitted Kalamata olives
$1\frac{1}{2}$ tsp chopped thyme or 1 tsp dried thyme
thyme and parsley leaves to garnish

METHOD
1 Season the lamb steaks with salt and pepper. Heat the olive oil in the casserole over medium-high heat. In batches, brown the meat on both sides. Transfer to a plate.

2 Meanwhile, pulse the onion, garlic, and chili in a food processor until it forms a coarse paste. Add to the casserole and reduce the heat to medium-low. Cook, stirring often, for 5 minutes. Stir in the wine, then the tomatoes and thyme. Bring to a simmer over high heat.

3 Return the lamb to the casserole. Reduce the heat to low and cover. Simmer until the lamb is very tender, about 45 minutes. During the last few minutes of cooking, stir in the olives. Season with salt and pepper.

4 Serve hot, sprinkled with thyme and parsley.

GOOD WITH Couscous cooked in vegetable stock.

PREPARE AHEAD The braise will be even better if refrigerated for at least 1 day and up to 3 days. To serve, let stand at room temperature for 1 hour, then reheat over low heat for 30 minutes, until hot.

6 servings

prep 20 mins
• cook 1½ hrs

large flame-
proof casserole
with a lid

freeze for up to
1 month

105

Navarin of lamb

Lighter than many stews, navarin contains lamb and young spring vegetables.

INGREDIENTS

1 tbsp butter
1 tbsp olive oil
2lb (900g) boneless shoulder of lamb,
   cut into 1½in (3.5cm) pieces
2 small onions, quartered
1 tbsp all-purpose flour
1½ cups lamb stock or beef stock
2 tbsp tomato paste
1 bouquet garni of 1 celery stalk,
   2 bay leaves, and 1 sprig of thyme
salt and freshly ground black pepper
10oz (300g) small new potatoes
10oz (300g) baby carrots
10oz (300g) baby turnips
6oz (175g) green beans

METHOD

1 Melt the butter with the oil in the casserole over medium-high heat. In batches, add the lamb and cook, turning occasionally, about 5 minutes, or until browned. Set aside. Cook the onions in the casserole until they begin to soften.

2 Return the lamb to the casserole. Sprinkle with the flour and stir well for 1 minute. Stir in the stock, then add the tomato paste and bouquet garni. Season with salt and pepper. Bring to a boil and cover. Simmer for 1 hour 15 minutes.

3 Stir in the potatoes, carrots, and turnips and cook, covered, for 15 minutes. Stir in the beans, cover, and cook for another 15 minutes, until the lamb and vegetables are tender.

GOOD WITH Lots of crusty French bread for soaking up the stew.

PREPARE AHEAD Cook through step 2, then cool, cover, and refrigerate for up to 1 day. Bring to a boil and finish the recipe.

4 servings

prep 30 mins • cook 1½ hrs

large flame-proof casserole

freeze for up to 3 months

Irish stew

There are many versions of this dish, all of which are based on lamb and potatoes. This one is a hearty casserole.

INGREDIENTS

3 large baking potatoes, peeled and thickly sliced
2lb (900g) boneless lamb shoulder,
    cut into 1½in (3.5cm) pieces
3 large onions, sliced
3 carrots, thickly sliced
salt and freshly ground black pepper
large sprig of thyme
1 bay leaf
2½ cups lamb stock or beef stock

METHOD

1 Preheat the oven to 325°F (160°C). Beginning and ending with potatoes, layer the lamb, onions, and carrots in a large, heavy casserole, seasoning each layer with salt and pepper. Tuck in the thyme and bay leaf. Add the stock and cover.

2 Bake for 1 hour. Uncover and bake 30–40 minutes more, until the potatoes are browned and the meat is very tender. Serve hot.

GOOD WITH A fresh green vegetable, such as kale or broccoli.

PREPARE AHEAD The stew can be made up to 2 days ahead, cooled, covered, and refrigerated. Reheat thoroughly in the oven before serving.

4–6 servings

**prep 20 mins
• cook 1 hr
30–40 mins**

Thai red beef curry

Thai curry paste is sold at Asian markets and some supermarkets.

INGREDIENTS

1lb (450g) sirloin steak,
  thinly sliced along the grain
3 tbsp vegetable oil
1 large garlic clove, minced
½ onion, thinly sliced
1 red bell pepper, seeded and thinly sliced
7oz (200g) white mushrooms, sliced
1½ tbsp Thai red curry paste
2 cups canned coconut milk
1½ tbsp Asian fish sauce
1 tbsp light brown sugar
4oz (115g) baby spinach leaves
3 tbsp shredded Thai basil leaves

METHOD

1 Toss the beef, 1 tbsp of the oil, and the garlic together. Heat a large wok over high heat. In batches, add the beef and stir-fry for 30 seconds to 1 minute, until the beef starts to change color. Using a slotted spoon, transfer to a plate.

2 When all the beef has been stir-fried, add the remaining oil to the wok and heat until shimmering. Add the onion and pepper and stir-fry for 2 minutes. Add the mushrooms and stir for 2 minutes more, or until all the vegetables are tender.

3 Stir in the curry paste. Add the coconut milk, fish sauce, and sugar and bring to a boil, stirring. Reduce the heat to medium and return the beef to the pan, along with the spinach and basil. Cook, stirring often, for 3 minutes, or until the beef is heated through and the spinach has wilted.

GOOD WITH Steamed rice.

4 servings

prep 20 mins
• cook 15 mins

110

Blanquette de veau

A simple, delicately flavored French veal stew in white sauce.

INGREDIENTS

1½lb (675g) boneless veal shoulder,
   cut into 2in (5cm) pieces
2 onions, chopped
2 carrots, chopped
2 tbsp fresh lemon juice
1 bouquet garni (6 parsley stalks, 1 celery rib,
   1 bay leaf, 5 black peppercorns,
   3 fresh thyme sprigs, tied in cheesecloth)
salt and freshly ground black pepper
6 tbsp butter
16 white pearl onions, peeled
8oz (225g) cremini mushrooms, quartered
2 tbsp all-purpose flour
3 tbsp heavy cream
1 large egg yolk
chopped parsley, to garnish

METHOD

1 Combine the veal, onions, carrots, lemon juice, and bouquet garni in the casserole and season with salt and pepper. Add enough water to cover. Bring to a boil over medium heat. Reduce the heat to low and simmer about 1 hour, or until the meat is tender.

2 Meanwhile, melt 2 tbsp of the butter in a frying pan over medium heat. Add the pearl onions and cook, stirring occasionally, about 5 minutes, until lightly browned. Add 2 tbsp of the remaining butter and the mushrooms. Cook, stirring occasionally, for 5 minutes, or until the mushrooms are tender.

3 Strain the stew, reserving 2¼ cups of the cooking liquid. Add the meat and vegetables to the mushroom mixture and cover.

4 Melt the remaining butter in a saucepan over medium-low heat. Whisk in the flour and cook for 1 minute. Whisk in the cooking liquid. Bring to a boil, whisking often.

5 Whisk the cream and egg yolks in a bowl, and gradually whisk in 1 cup of the sauce. Return to the saucepan. Pour the sauce over the meat and heat without boiling, stirring gently. Sprinkle with the parsley and serve hot.

GOOD WITH Steamed rice.

4 servings

prep 15 mins
• cook 1½ hrs

large
flame-proof
casserole

Meat loaf

This recipe is great served hot for a weekday family meal, or cold in a sandwich or packed lunch.

INGREDIENTS
vegetable oil, for the pan
12oz (340g) ground beef round
8oz (225g) ground pork
1 onion, finely chopped
⅓ cup packed fresh bread crumbs
2 tbsp chopped parsley
2 tsp spicy brown mustard
1 tsp paprika
salt and freshly ground black pepper
1 large egg, beaten
3 hard-boiled eggs, peeled

For the sauce
½ cup sour cream
3 small sour pickles (cornichons), chopped
1 tbsp capers, chopped
1 tbsp finely chopped parsley

METHOD
1 Preheat the oven to 400°F (200°C). Lightly oil an 8 x 4in (20 x 10cm) loaf pan.

2 Mix together the ground beef, pork, onion, bread crumbs, parsley, mustard, and paprika and season with salt and pepper. Stir in the beaten egg and mix thoroughly.

3 Evenly spread half of the mixture in the pan. Arrange the hard-boiled eggs down the center, then top with the remaining meat mixture and smooth the top.

4 Cover the loaf pan with aluminum foil. Bake for about 50 minutes, until firm. Let stand for 10 minutes before turning out onto a warmed platter.

5 To make the sauce, mix the sour cream, pickles, capers, and parsley.

6 Serve the meat loaf cut into slices, with the sauce spooned over and extra on the side.

GOOD WITH A salad of arugula and halved cherry tomatoes.

PREPARE AHEAD The loaf can be prepared through step 4 and refrigerated for up to 8 hours. The sauce can be covered and refrigerated for up to 3 days.

4 servings

prep 20 mins
• cook 30 mins

loaf pan

Watercress and pear soup

For extra flavor, serve this velvety soup with shredded Parmesan cheese.

INGREDIENTS
2 tbsp butter
1 onion, finely chopped
6oz (175g) watercress
3 ripe pears, peeled, cored, and roughly chopped
1qt (liter) chicken stock
salt and freshly ground black pepper
3/4 cup heavy cream
1 tbsp fresh lemon juice
olive oil, to drizzle

METHOD
1 Melt the butter in a large saucepan over medium-low heat. Add the onion and cover. Cook, stirring occasionally, about 10 minutes, or until tender.

2 Meanwhile, trim the watercress and pluck off the leaves. Add the watercress stems to the pot with the pears and stock. Bring to a boil over high heat.

3 Cover and simmer gently for 15 minutes, or until the pears are tender. Season with salt and pepper. Reserving a few watercress leaves for garnish, purée the soup and watercress leaves in a blender. Add the cream and lemon juice, and adjust the seasoning.

4 Serve hot, garnished with watercress leaves.

PREPARE AHEAD The soup can cooled, covered, and refrigerated up to one day.

4 servings

**prep 10 mins
• cook 15 mins**

**the soup,
without the
cream, can
be frozen up
to 3 months**

Stracciatella with pasta

A simple combination of chicken broth with eggs.

INGREDIENTS
6 cups chicken stock, preferably homemade
salt and freshly ground black pepper
1 cup small pasta, such as ditalini or broken spaghetti
4 large eggs
$\frac{1}{2}$ tsp freshly grated nutmeg
1 tbsp chopped parsley
1 tbsp butter

METHOD
1 Bring the stock to a steady boil. Season with salt and pepper. Add the pasta and cook according to package instructions.

2 Beat the eggs with the nutmeg, and season with salt and pepper. Add the parsley.

3 Reduce the heat to low. Add the butter to the stock. Stir the simmering stock with a whisk so the stock swirls in a vortex. In a steady stream, add the eggs. Cook about 1 minute, until the egg strands look set. Do not let the stock return to a boil. Remove from the heat and let stand for 3 minutes. Serve hot.

4–6 servings

prep 10 mins
• cook 20 mins

Pasta alla carbonara

A popular Italian classic. Use the freshest eggs possible and serve the pasta just after you have tossed it.

INGREDIENTS

1lb (450g) dried pasta, such as spaghetti or tagliatelle
4 tbsp olive oil
6oz (175g) pancetta, very finely chopped
2 garlic cloves, minced
5 large eggs
1/2 cup freshly grated Parmesan
1/2 cup freshly grated Romano, plus more to serve
freshly ground black pepper

METHOD

1 Bring a large saucepan of salted water to the boil over high heat. Add the pasta, stir, and cook according to the package instructions, until *al dente*.

2 Meanwhile, heat the oil in a large frying pan over medium heat. Add the pancetta and cook, stirring occasionally, about 6 minutes, until crispy. Add the garlic and cook for 1 minute.

3 Beat the eggs, Parmesan, and Romano together and season with pepper. Drain the pasta well and return to its saucepan. Add the egg mixture and the contents of the pan with the pancetta, including the fat, and mix quickly until the pasta is well coated. Serve immediately, with extra Romano passed on the side.

GOOD WITH A simple salad.

4–6 servings

prep 10 mins
• cook 10 mins

Singapore noodles

This popular dish combines the delicacy of Chinese cooking, the heat of Indian spices, and the fragrance of Malaysian herbs.

INGREDIENTS

6oz (175g) thin Asian egg noodles
2 tbsp plus 1 tsp vegetable oil
5oz (140g) boneless skinless chicken breast, thinly sliced
5oz (140g) medium shrimp, peeled
1 onion, thinly sliced
½ red bell pepper, cored, seeded, and cut into strips
1 small head of bok choy, sliced
2 garlic cloves, finely chopped
1 fresh hot red chili, seeded and minced
4oz (115g) bean sprouts
2 tbsp light soy sauce
1 tbsp curry powder
2 large eggs, beaten
cilantro leaves, for garnish

METHOD

1 Bring a large pot of lightly salted water to a boil over high heat. Add the noodles and cook until tender. Drain and rinse under cold water. Toss with 1 tsp of the oil.

2 Heat 1 tbsp oil in a wok over high heat. Add the chicken and stir-fry for 1 minute. Add the shrimp and stir-fry for another 2 minutes. Transfer to a plate.

3 Add 1 tbsp oil to the wok and heat. Add the onion and stir-fry for 2 minutes. Add the pepper, bok choy, garlic, and chili, and stir-fry for 2 minutes more. Add the bean sprouts and stir-fry for 2 minutes.

4 Add the soy sauce and curry powder and stir-fry for 1 minute. Add the noodles, pour in the eggs, and toss together until the egg starts to set. Return the chicken and shrimp to the wok and stir-fry for 1 minute. Sprinkle with cilantro and serve hot.

PREPARE AHEAD Slice the chicken, chop the vegetables, and peel the shrimp and refrigerate for up to 8 hours before cooking.

4 servings

prep 15 mins
• cook 10 mins

low fat

cook the shrimp
on the day of
purchase

wok

Quinoa tabbouleh

Whole grain quinoa makes a tasty and healthy summer salad. Be sure to rinse it well in a fine sieve before cooking.

INGREDIENTS
1 cup quinoa
1 cucumber, peeled, seeded, and diced
1 small red onion, chopped
2 tbsp chopped parsley
2 tbsp chopped mint
salt and freshly ground black pepper
$\frac{1}{2}$ cup olive oil
2 tbsp fresh lemon juice
2oz (60g) feta cheese
$\frac{1}{2}$ cup pitted and coarsely chopped Kalamata olives

METHOD
1 Rinse the quinoa well in a fine mesh sieve. Drain and place it in a medium heavy-bottomed pan. Stir constantly over a medium heat about 3 minutes, until the grains separate and begin to brown.

2 Add 2$\frac{1}{4}$ cups water and $\frac{1}{2}$ tsp salt and bring to a boil over high heat. Reduce the heat and cook for 15 minutes, or until the liquid is absorbed. Transfer to a bowl and let cool.

3 Add the cucumber, onion, parsley, and mint to the quinoa. Whisk together the oil and lemon juice in a small bowl. Pour over the quinoa and mix.

4 Sprinkle with the feta cheese and olives. Season with salt and pepper, and serve.

4 servings

prep 10 mins
• cook 20 mins

Puy lentils with goat cheese, olives, and fresh thyme

French Puy lentils hold their shape during cooking and lend an attractive look to rustic lentil recipes.

INGREDIENTS

$1^2/_3$ cups Puy lentils, rinsed
1 carrot, peeled and diced
1 shallot or small onion, finely chopped
2 sprigs of thyme
1 bay leaf
$3/_4$ cup pitted and chopped Kalamata olives
3oz (85g) rindless goat cheese, crumbled
2 tbsp extra virgin olive oil
salt and freshly ground black pepper
6oz (170g) mixed baby salad leaves, to serve (optional)

METHOD

1 Place the lentils, carrot, shallot, thyme, and bay leaf in a saucepan with 5 cups of water. Simmer for 15–20 minutes or until the lentils are tender.

2 Drain the lentils well, transfer to a serving bowl, and remove the thyme and bay leaf. Cool until lukewarm. Add the olives, goat cheese, and olive oil, and stir together. Season with salt and pepper and serve warm.

GOOD WITH Grilled spicy sausages, lamb chops, or pork chops.

PREPARE AHEAD The lentils can be cooked ahead in step 1 and reheated, or the dish can be served chilled as a salad.

4–6 servings

prep 10 mins
• cook 30 mins

Piperade

This savory scrambled egg dish is from the Basque region of southwest France.

INGREDIENTS

2 tbsp olive oil
1 large onion, chopped
1 red bell pepper, seeded and chopped
1 green bell pepper, seeded and chopped
2 garlic cloves, minced
3oz (85g) Serrano ham or prosciutto, chopped
4 ripe medium tomatoes, peeled, seeded, and chopped
8 large eggs
salt and freshly ground black pepper
2 tbsp chopped parsley

METHOD

1 Heat the oil in a large frying pan over medium heat. Add the onion and cook about 3 minutes, until beginning to soften. Add the red and green peppers and garlic and cook, stirring occasionally, until the peppers soften, about 5 minutes.

2 Add the ham and cook for 2 minutes. Add the tomatoes and cook for about 7 minutes, or until the juices evaporate.

3 Beat the eggs and season with salt and pepper. Pour into the pan and cook until scrambled, stirring often. Sprinkle with parsley and serve.

4 servings

**prep 5 mins
• cook 20 mins**

Finnan haddie with spinach and pancetta

Some stores carry this deeply smoked fish for a quick supper.

INGREDIENTS

1 tbsp olive oil
1 tbsp butter, plus more for the dish
1 onion, finely chopped
3oz (85g) sliced pancetta or bacon, chopped
1lb (450g) spinach leaves, washed
$\frac{1}{2}$ cup crème fraîche or heavy cream
$\frac{1}{2}$ cup freshly grated Parmesan
salt and freshly ground black pepper
1$\frac{3}{4}$lb (800g) finnan haddie (smoked haddock), skinned
juice of $\frac{1}{2}$ lemon
$\frac{1}{2}$ cup fresh bread crumbs

METHOD

1 Preheat the oven to 375°F (190°C). Butter an oven-proof serving dish. Melt the oil and butter together in a frying pan over medium-high heat. Add the onion and pancetta and cook until lightly browned, about 5 minutes.

2 In batches, stir in the spinach and cook until wilted. Stir in the crème fraîche and 6 tbsp of the Parmesan. Season with salt and pepper and simmer until it has thickened slightly.

3 Spoon the spinach mixture into the dish. Place the finnan haddie on top. Sprinkle with lemon juice. Mix the bread crumbs and remaining 2 tbsp Parmesan and sprinkle over the fish. Bake for 15–20 minutes, or until the fish is hot.

6 servings

prep 10 mins
• cook 15–20 mins

Seafood curry

This quick curry is flavored with chilies, coconut, and lime.

INGREDIENTS

20oz (600g) skinless white fish fillets,
    such as cod or haddock, cut into bite-sized pieces,
    rinsed and patted dry
$\frac{1}{2}$ tsp salt
$\frac{1}{2}$ tsp ground turmeric
$\frac{1}{2}$ onion, chopped
1 tbsp peeled and chopped fresh ginger
1 garlic clove, minced
2 tbsp vegetable oil
1 tsp black mustard seeds
4 green cardamom pods, lightly crushed
2–4 dried red chilies, lightly crushed
2 cups canned coconut milk
12 large shrimp, peeled and deveined
2 tbsp fresh lime juice
salt and freshly ground black pepper
cilantro leaves and lemon wedges, to garnish

METHOD

1 Put the fish in a nonmetallic bowl. Sprinkle with the salt and turmeric. Set aside.

2 Purée the onion, ginger, and garlic in a blender or a food processor. Heat a large wok or deep frying pan over high heat until hot. Add the oil and swirl it to coat the bottom of the pan. Reduce the heat to medium. Add the mustard seeds, cardamom pods, and chili and stir until the mustard seeds sputter and "jump." Add the onion paste and cook, stirring often, for 3 minutes until it just begins to color.

3 Stir in the coconut milk. Boil for 2 minutes. Reduce the heat to medium-low and add the fish, with any juices in the bowl. Spoon the sauce over the fish and simmer for 2 minutes, occasionally basting the fish with the sauce, taking care not to break up fish.

4 Add the shrimp to the pan and simmer for 2 minutes more, or until the shrimp turn opaque and the fish flakes easily. Add the lime juice and season to taste with salt and pepper. Serve hot, garnished with the cilantro leaves and lemon wedges.

4 servings

**prep 15 mins
• cook 10–12 mins**

Thai green chicken curry

Use Thai curry paste, available at Asian markets and many supermarkets, to make this quick and flavorful dish.

INGREDIENTS

1 tbsp vegetable oil
4 skinless, boneless chicken breasts,
    about 5oz (140g) each,
    cut into bite-sized pieces
4 tsp Thai green or red curry paste
    (or more for a spicier sauce)
14fl oz (400ml) can coconut milk
2 tbsp soy sauce
4 large white button mushrooms,
    wiped and chopped
6 scallions, trimmed, green part only,
    cut into 1/4in (5mm) slices
salt and freshly ground black pepper
chopped cilantro, to garnish

METHOD

1 Heat the oil in a large frying pan over medium heat. Add the chicken and stir-fry for 2 minutes, or until browned. Stir in the curry paste.

2 Add the coconut milk and soy sauce and bring to a boil, stirring often. Reduce the heat, and stir in the mushrooms and most of the scallions. Simmer for about 8 minutes, or until the chicken is tender and the juices run clear when pierced with the point of a knife. Season with salt and pepper.

3 Serve hot, garnished with the cilantro and remaining scallions.

GOOD WITH A bowl of long-grain rice or plain noodles.

PREPARE AHEAD This dish can be cooked in advance and reheated.

4 servings

prep 10 mins
• cook 10 mins

137

Deviled turkey

Serve these spicy stir-fried turkey strips as a healthy lunch or supper.

INGREDIENTS

2 tbsp olive oil

1lb (450g) turkey breast cutlets, cut into strips

1 onion, finely chopped

1 red bell pepper, seeded and cut into strips

1 orange bell pepper, seeded and cut into strips

1 garlic clove, minced

3 tbsp fresh orange juice

2 tbsp whole grain mustard

2 tbsp mango chutney

¼ tsp sweet paprika

2 tbsp Worcestershire sauce

1 fresh hot red chili, seeded and minced

METHOD

1 Heat the oil in a nonstick frying pan over a high heat. Add the turkey and cook, stirring often, about 5 minutes, until lightly browned. Transfer to a plate.

2 Add the onion and stir-fry about 2 minutes, or until it is just beginning to color. Add the red and orange peppers and garlic and stir-fry about 3 minutes.

3 Mix the orange juice, mustard, chutney, paprika, Worcestershire sauce, and chili together until well combined. Stir into the vegetables and return the turkey to the pan. Cook about 5 minutes or until piping hot and the turkey is opaque throughout. Serve hot.

GOOD WITH Stir-fried spinach and rice or noodles.

4 servings

prep 10 mins
• cook 15 mins

Quick lamb curry

Use leftover lamb for this dish and adjust the spiciness of the sauce with the amount of curry powder.

INGREDIENTS

2 green bell peppers, seeded and quartered
1 onion, quartered
3 garlic cloves, sliced
one 1in (2.5cm) piece fresh ginger,
    peeled and chopped
2 tbsp vegetable oil
1 tbsp black mustard seeds
1 tbsp curry powder
one 14.5oz (411g) can chopped tomatoes
$\frac{1}{2}$ cup canned coconut milk
4 cups (bite-sized pieces) cooked lamb
1 cup frozen peas
salt and freshly ground black pepper
chopped cilantro, to garnish

METHOD

1 Purée the green peppers, onion, garlic, and ginger with 1 tbsp water in a blender.

2 Heat 1 tbsp of the oil in a large saucepan over medium-high heat. Add the mustard seeds and cook, stirring frequently, for about 30 seconds, or until they begin to pop. Pour in the onion purée and cook, stirring often, for about 3 minutes, until the purée is thick and fairly dry.

3 Add the remaining 1 tbsp oil and the curry powder and stir for 30 seconds. Stir in the tomatoes with their juice and cook for 1 minute, stirring often, then stir in the coconut milk and mix well.

4 Add the lamb and peas and return to a boil. Reduce the heat to low and cover. Simmer for about 6 minutes, until the peas are tender. Season with salt and pepper. Garnish with the cilantro and serve hot.

GOOD WITH Rice or naan bread, or as part of a feast with other curries.

4 servings

prep 15 mins
• cook 25 mins

freeze for up to
3 months

140

Chinese chili beef stir-fry

This hot stir-fry is best when the meat has time to marinate. But for super quick results, first coat and fry.

INGREDIENTS

3 tbsp soy sauce, preferably dark sauce
2 tbsp rice vinegar
1 tsp Chinese five spice powder
1lb (450g) beef round steak, cut into thin strips
freshly ground black pepper
4 tbsp vegetable oil
$\frac{1}{2}$ red bell pepper, seeded and thinly sliced
1 fresh hot red chili, seeded and finely chopped
1 garlic clove, crushed and chopped
1 tsp peeled and grated fresh ginger
1 cup broccoli florets
1 cup snow peas
1 tsp cornstarch
$\frac{1}{2}$ cup beef stock
few drops of Asian sesame oil

METHOD

1 Mix the soy sauce, vinegar, and five spice powder together in a bowl. Add the beef and toss well. Season well with black pepper. Cover and refrigerate for at least 2 and up to 12 hours.

2 Heat 2 tbsp oil in a wok over high heat. Add the bell pepper and stir-fry until crisp and tender, about 3 minutes. Add the chili, garlic, and ginger and stir-fry for 1 minute. Add the broccoli and snow peas and stir-fry for 2 minutes. Transfer to a platter.

3 Add the remaining oil to the wok and heat over high heat. Drain the beef from the marinade, reserving the marinade. Add the beef to the wok and stir-fry for 1 minute. Return the vegetables to the wok and pour in the marinade. Dissolve the cornstarch in the stock, and stir into the wok. Stir-fry the steak and vegetables until the sauce is boiling.

4 Transfer to a plate, drizzle with the sesame oil, and serve at once.

4 servings

**prep 15 mins,
plus marinating
• cook 10 mins**

**low GI if served
with extra stir-fry
vegetables
rather than
rice or noodles**

wok

Soufflé omelet

Beaten egg whites give this omelet a light and fluffy texture.

INGREDIENTS
2 large eggs, separated
salt and freshly ground black pepper
1 tbsp butter
¼ cup shredded sharp Cheddar
¼ cup shredded Gruyère
1oz (30g) sliced ham, cut into strips
chopped chives, for garnish

METHOD
1 Preheat the broiler. Whisk the egg whites in a bowl until soft peaks form. Whisk the egg yolks in a bowl until pale and lightly thickened. Whisk in 2 tbsp water and season with salt and pepper. Add the whites to the yolks. Add 2 tbsp each of the Cheddar and Gruyère and fold together with a rubber spatula just until combined.

2 Heat the butter in an 7in (18cm) nonstick frying pan over medium heat until the butter is foaming. Add the egg mixture and spread evenly. Cook for about 1 minute, until the eggs look set around the edges. Run a heatproof spatula around the edge of the omelet to loosen it.

3 Sprinkle with the remaining Cheddar and Gruyère and the ham. Broil about 1 minute, until the top of the omelet is set. Run the spatula around the edge of omelet. Fold the omelet almost in half and slide onto the plate. Sprinkle with the chives and serve hot.

GOOD WITH Toast and grilled tomatoes.

1 serving

**prep 10 mins
• cook 5 mins**

**nonstick
frying pan**

Sauté of liver, bacon, and shallots

Quick to cook, tender calves' liver is the perfect partner to salty bacon and is served here in a rich sauce.

INGREDIENTS
12oz (350g) calves' liver
8 thick bacon slices, preferably maple cured
1 tbsp olive oil
2 tbsp butter
4 shallots, thinly sliced
$^2/_3$ cup dry vermouth
1 tsp Dijon mustard
dash of Worcestershire sauce (optional)
salt and freshly ground black pepper

METHOD
1 Cut the liver and the bacon into strips about 2in (6cm) long and $^1/_2$in (1.5cm) wide.

2 Heat 1 tbsp each oil and butter in a large frying pan over medium heat. Add the shallots and cook, stirring frequently, for 5 minutes, or until golden. Transfer to a plate.

3 Add the remaining oil and butter to the pan and increase the heat to high. Add the liver and bacon and cook for 3–4 minutes, until the liver is seared and slightly pink inside.

4 Return the shallots to the pan. Pour in the vermouth, and boil, scraping up any browned bits in the pan with a wooden spoon for 1–2 minutes.

5 Reduce the heat to medium-low and stir in the mustard and the Worcestershire sauce (if using). Season with salt and pepper and serve at once.

GOOD WITH Mashed potatoes and green beans for a tasty supper dish.

4 servings

prep 10 mins
• cook 10 mins

Tomato soup

Easy to make using canned tomatoes, this delicious soup can be enjoyed all year round.

INGREDIENTS

1 tbsp olive oil
1 onion, chopped
2 celery stalks, sliced
1 garlic clove, sliced
1 carrot, sliced
1 baking potato, peeled and chopped
one 28oz (784g) can plum tomatoes in juice
3 cups vegetable or chicken stock
1 tsp sugar
1 bay leaf
salt and freshly ground black pepper

METHOD

1 Heat the oil in a large saucepan over medium-low heat. Add the onion, celery, and garlic. Cook, stirring frequently, until softened but not colored.

2 Add the carrot and potato and stir for 1 minute. Add the tomatoes with their juice, the stock, sugar, and bay leaf. Season to taste with salt and pepper. Bring to a boil over high heat, then return the heat to medium-low. Cover and simmer for 45 minutes, or until the vegetables are very tender.

3 Let cool slightly. In batches, purée in a blender with the lid ajar. Adjust the seasoning. Reheat gently and serve hot.

GOOD WITH A swirl of heavy cream, crème fraîche, or yogurt, or a garnish of celery leaves.

PREPARE AHEAD The soup can be cooled and refrigerated for up to 2 days.

6–8 servings

prep 20 mins • cook 55 mins

low fat

Carrot and orange soup

A light, refreshing soup with a hint of spice, this is the perfect start to a summer meal.

INGREDIENTS

1lb (450g) carrots, sliced
1 leek, white and pale green parts only, sliced
2 tsp olive oil
1 small baking potato, about 4oz (115g),
   peeled and chopped
1/2 tsp ground coriander
pinch of ground cumin
10fl oz (300ml) orange juice
2 cups vegetable or chicken stock
1 bay leaf
salt and freshly ground black pepper
2 tbsp chopped cilantro, to garnish

METHOD

1 Combine the carrots, leek, and oil in a large saucepan and cook over low heat, stirring frequently for 5 minutes, or until the leeks have softened. Stir in the potato, coriander, and cumin. Add the stock, orange juice, and bay leaf and stir well.

2 Increase the heat to high and bring to a boil. Return the heat to low and cover. Simmer about 40 minutes, until the vegetables are very tender.

3 Let cool slightly. In batches, purée in a blender with the lid ajar. Return to the saucepan and season with salt and pepper. If the soup is too thick, thin with a little water. Ladle into soup bowls, garnished with the cilantro.

GOOD WITH A spoonful of low-fat plain yogurt or a swirl of cream.

PREPARE AHEAD The soup can be made up to 2 days in advance.

4 servings

**prep 10 mins
• cook 40 mins**

low fat

Lentil soup

This hearty vegetarian soup has just a hint of spice certain to warm you up.

INGREDIENTS

1 tbsp olive oil
2 onions, finely chopped
2 celery stalks, finely chopped
2 carrots, finely chopped
2 garlic cloves, crushed
1–2 tsp curry powder
5½ cups vegetable stock
¾ cup red lentils
½ cup tomato or multi-vegetable juice
salt and freshly ground black pepper

METHOD

1 Heat the oil in a large saucepan set over medium heat. Add the onions, celery, and carrots. Cook, stirring frequently, for about 5 minutes, or until the onions are translucent.

2 Add the garlic and curry powder and cook, stirring, for 1 minute more. Add the stock, lentils, and tomato juice.

3 Bring to a boil. Reduce the heat to medium-low and cover. Simmer for 25 minutes, or until the lentils are tender. Season to taste with salt and pepper and serve hot.

GOOD WITH A spoonful of plain yogurt and crusty bread.

4–6 servings

prep 20 mins
• cook 35 mins

low fat

Lentil salad with lemon and almonds

Preserved lemons are available at Mediterranean grocers.

INGREDIENTS

1³/₄ cups French green (Puy) lentils,
   rinsed and drained
2 tbsp sherry vinegar
6 tbsp extra virgin olive oil
1 cup loosely packed cilantro leaves
2 preserved lemon quarters,
   rinsed and finely chopped
1 shallot, minced
salt and freshly ground black pepper
3 tbsp butter
³/₄ cup slivered almonds

METHOD

1 Bring the lentils with enough cold water to cover to a boil in a medium saucepan over high heat. Reduce the heat to medium-low and simmer about 15 minutes until tender. Drain, rinse under cold water, and let cool.

2 Whisk the vinegar and oil in a bowl. Add the lentils, ¹/₂ cup of cilantro, the preserved lemons, and half of the shallot. Season with salt and pepper.

3 Melt the butter in a small frying pan over medium heat. Add the almonds and cook, stirring often, until golden brown. Drain and cool on paper towels. Stir the almonds into the lentil salad. Let stand for 10 minutes or so to let the flavors blend.

4 Scatter the remaining onion and cilantro over the salad and serve at room temperature.

GOOD WITH Grilled lamb chops, or with firm oily fish, such as swordfish or mackerel.

PREPARE AHEAD The salad can be prepared several hours in advance. Cover and refrigerate until ready to serve.

4 servings

**prep 10 mins,
plus standing
• cook 15–20
mins**

Kasha with vegetables

Kasha, also called buckwheat groats, is a healthy and delicious whole grain cereal that can be prepared in a manner similar to risotto to make a hearty vegetarian main course.

INGREDIENTS
2 tbsp olive oil
1 onion, finely chopped
1 carrot, finely chopped
2 portabella mushrooms, sliced
1 celery stalk, finely chopped
1 garlic clove, minced
$1/3$ cup kasha (buckwheat groats)
$1/2$ cup dry white wine
about $4\frac{1}{4}$ cups hot vegetable stock or water
1 beet, cooked until tender, chopped
2oz (55g) rindless goat cheese, crumbled
2 tbsp chopped parsley

METHOD
1 Heat the oil in a large saucepan over medium heat. Add the onion, carrot, mushrooms, celery, and garlic, and cook, stirring often, for 8–10 minutes, or until lightly browned. Add the kasha and cook, stirring often, for 2–3 minutes more. Add the wine and stir until it has been absorbed.

2 Stir in $1/2$ cup hot vegetable stock and reduce the heat to medium-low. Simmer, stirring, until the stock is absorbed. Stir in another $1/2$ cup of stock and repeat. Continue cooking and adding more stock for about 20 minutes, or until the kasha is tender but still chewy.

3 Stir in the beet and season with salt and pepper. Transfer to a serving bowl and sprinkle with cheese and parsley. Serve hot.

GOOD WITH Crusty bread, as a main meal.

4–6 servings

prep 5 mins
• cook 40 mins

Spaghetti mare e monti

This pasta dish combines ingredients from the sea (*mare*) and from the mountains (*monti*).

INGREDIENTS

$^1/_2$oz (15g) dried porcini mushrooms, rinsed
$^2/_3$ cup boiling water
2 tbsp extra-virgin olive oil
6oz (175g) white mushrooms
2 garlic cloves, minced
1 bay leaf
6 ripe plum tomatoes, peeled, seeded, and chopped
$^2/_3$ cup dry white wine
8oz (225g) medium shrimp, peeled and deveined
salt and freshly ground black pepper
1lb (450g) dried spaghetti

METHOD

1 Combine the porcini and boiling water in a bowl. Let stand for 30 minutes. Remove the mushrooms with a slotted spoon and chop them. Strain the soaking liquid through a fine sieve and reserve. Bring a large pot of salted water to a boil.

2 Heat the olive oil in a large frying pan over medium-high heat. Add the white mushrooms and cook, stirring often, about 5 minutes, until golden. Add the porcini and garlic and cook for 30 seconds. Pour in the porcini liquid, add the bay leaf, and simmer until the liquid is reduced to a glaze. Reduce the heat to low.

3 Add the tomatoes and wine and simmer for 7–8 minutes, until the liquid is slightly reduced and the tomatoes are beginning to break down. Remove the bay leaf. Add the shrimp and cook for 1 minute, or until just opaque. Season with salt and pepper.

4 When the sauce is almost done, cook the spaghetti in the boiling water according to the package directions until *al dente*. Drain well, then return to the pot. Add the sauce and toss well. Transfer to deep bowls and serve hot.

4–6 servings

**prep 15 mins,
plus soaking
• cook 15 mins**

**low in
saturated fat**

Chili tofu stir-fry

This quick and easy dish takes advantage of tofu's ability to take on other flavors.

INGREDIENTS
2 tbsp vegetable oil
¾ cup unsalted cashews
10oz (300g) firm tofu,
   cut into 1in (2.5cm) cubes
1 red onion, thinly sliced
2 carrots, thinly sliced
1 red bell pepper, seeded and chopped
1 celery stalk, chopped
4 cremini mushrooms, sliced
6oz (175g) bean sprouts
¾ cup vegetable or chicken stock
2 tbsp soy sauce
2 tsp Asian chili-garlic sauce
1 tsp cornstarch

METHOD
1 Heat the oil in a wok over high heat. Add the cashews and stir-fry for about 30 seconds or until lightly browned. Using a slotted spoon, transfer to paper towels.

2 Add the tofu and stir-fry about 2 minutes, or until golden. Transfer to the paper towels. Add the onion and carrots and stir-fry for 2 minutes, until crisp and tender; add the red pepper, celery, and mushrooms and stir-fry for 3 minutes more. Finally, add the bean sprouts and stir-fry for 2 minutes, until hot. Always keep the heat under the wok high so that the vegetables sear quickly without overcooking.

3 Meanwhile, mix the stock, soy sauce, and chili sauce in a small bowl. Add the cornstarch, and stir to dissolve. Return the cashews and tofu to the wok and add the stock mixture. Stir until the sauce is bubbling and lightly thickened. Serve hot.

GOOD WITH Boiled rice or Chinese-style egg noodles.

4 servings

prep 10 mins
• cook 15 mins

wok

Fideua

Think of this as a seafood paella made with pasta instead of rice.

INGREDIENTS

pinch of saffron threads
3 cups fish stock, heated, as needed
2 tbsp olive oil
1 onion, finely chopped
2 garlic cloves, minced
3 ripe tomatoes, skinned, seeded and chopped
1 tsp sweet paprika
10oz (300g) spaghetti or linguine,
  broken into 2in (5cm) lengths
8oz (225g) firm white fish fillets,
  such as cod, haddock, or monkfish,
  skinned and cut into $^3/_4$in (2cm) slices
8oz (225g) large shrimp, peeled and deveined
12 mussels or clams, scrubbed
8 small scallops, cut in half
1 cup frozen peas, thawed
salt and freshly ground black pepper
2 tbsp chopped parsley

METHOD

1 Combine the saffron and 2 tbsp of the fish stock in a small bowl. Set aside.

2 Heat the oil in a large frying pan over medium heat. Add the onion and garlic and cook, stirring often, for about 5 minutes, until translucent. Add the tomatoes and paprika and cook for 5 minutes. Add the pasta, 2 cups of the remaining stock, and the soaked saffron. Bring to a boil. Cook for 5 minutes.

3 Add the fish, shrimp, mussels, scallops, and peas to the frying pan. Continue cooking until the pasta is tender, adding more stock as needed to keep the mixture moist. Season with salt and pepper. Sprinkle with the parsley and serve directly from the pan.

GOOD WITH Chunks of crusty bread to mop up the juices.

4 servings

prep 15 mins
• cook 25 mins

low fat

Herb-baked swordfish

Rosemary is not usually used with fish, but it perfectly complements the meaty flavor of swordfish.

INGREDIENTS

4 swordfish steaks about 6oz (175g) each, skin removed
salt and freshly ground black pepper
2 tbsp extra virgin olive oil, plus more for the dish
1 fennel bulb, thinly sliced
4 ripe tomatoes, sliced
1 lemon, sliced
4 tbsp chopped parsley
1 tbsp chopped mint
2 tsp finely chopped rosemary
1 tsp chopped thyme
$\frac{1}{2}$ cup dry white wine

METHOD

1 Preheat the oven to 350°F (180°C). Season the swordfish with salt and pepper. Lightly oil a large baking dish. Spread the fennel in the dish and season with salt and pepper.

2 Place the swordfish in the dish in a single layer. Top with the tomato and lemon. Mix the parsley, mint, rosemary, and thyme together, and sprinkle over the fish. Pour the wine and the oil over the fish. Cover with aluminum foil.

3 Bake for 15–20 minutes, or until the fish look opaque when flaked with a knife. Serve immediately, with the pan juices.

GOOD WITH Steamed new potatoes and green vegetables, such as broccoli or green beans.

4 servings

prep 20 mins
• cook 15–20 mins

low fat

Chicken and chickpea pilaf

This one-pot rice dish is full of flavor and is easy to make.

INGREDIENTS

pinch of saffron threads
2 tbsp vegetable oil
6 skinless and boneless chicken thighs,
  cut into small pieces
salt and freshly ground black pepper
2 tsp ground coriander
1 tsp ground cumin
1 onion, sliced
1 red pepper, seeded and chopped
2 garlic cloves, peeled and crushed
1¼ cups long-grain rice
2½ cups hot chicken stock
2 bay leaves
one 15oz (420g) can chickpeas
⅓ cup golden raisins
½ cup slivered almonds toasted
3 tbsp chopped parsley

METHOD

1 Crumble the saffron threads into a small bowl, add 2 tbsp boiling water, and set aside for at least 10 minutes.

2 Meanwhile, heat 1 tbsp oil in a large saucepan over medium heat. Season the chicken with salt and pepper and sprinkle with the coriander and cumin. In batches, cook the chicken, stirring often, for 3 minutes. Transfer to a plate. Add the remaining oil to the saucepan and heat. Add the onion, red pepper, and garlic and cook, stirring often, about 5 minutes, until softened.

3 Stir in the rice. Return the chicken to the saucepan and stir in the stock, along with the saffron and its liquid, ½ tsp salt, and the bay leaves. Bring to a boil over high heat. Reduce the heat to low and cover. Simmer for 15 minutes. Rinse and drain the chickpeas then stir in along with the raisins, and cook about 5 minutes, or until the rice is tender. Remove from the heat and let stand, covered, for 5 minutes. Transfer to a warm serving platter and serve hot, sprinkled with almonds and parsley.

4 servings

prep 20 mins
• cook 35 mins

low fat

Boeuf bourguignon

Long, slow braising allows the beef to absorb the rich flavors of the wine and herbs and tenderizes it in the process.

INGREDIENTS

6oz (175g) sliced bacon, chopped
2 tbsp vegetable oil
2lb (900g) beef chuck, cut into 1½in (4cm) cubes
salt and freshly ground black pepper
12 small shallots, peeled
1 tbsp all-purpose flour
1¼ cups red wine, preferably Pinot Noir
1¼ cups beef stock
4oz (115g) white mushrooms, quartered
1 tsp dried *herbes de Provence*
1 bay leaf
3 tbsp chopped parsley

METHOD

1 Preheat the oven to 325°F (160°C). Cook the bacon in a flame-proof casserole over medium heat until lightly browned. Transfer to paper towels to drain.

2 Add 1 tbsp oil to the casserole and increase the heat to medium-high. Season the beef with salt and pepper. In batches, add the beef and cook, turning occasionally, about 5 minutes, or until browned. Transfer to a plate.

3 Meanwhile, heat the remaining 1 tbsp oil in a frying pan over medium heat. Add the shallots and cook, stirring, until lightly browned, about 5 minutes.

4 Return the beef to the casserole. Sprinkle with flour and stir well. Stir in the wine and stock and bring to a boil over high heat. Add the shallots, mushrooms, bacon, herbs, and bay leaf, and cover. Bake for about 2 hours until the meat is very tender.

5 Sprinkle with chopped parsley, and serve.

GOOD WITH Mashed potatoes, buttered baby carrots, and broccoli or green beans.

PREPARE AHEAD This stew can made up to 2 days ahead, cooled, covered, and refrigerated. Reheat in a 350°F (180°C) oven for 30 minutes.

4–6 servings

prep 25 mins
• cook 2½ hrs

low GI

freeze for up to
3 months

Arroz con pollo

This one-dish chicken and rice meal is served wherever there are Spanish-speaking cooks.

INGREDIENTS

2 tbsp olive oil
8 chicken thighs
1 onion, finely sliced
1 green and 1 red bell pepper, both seeded and chopped
2 garlic cloves, finely chopped
one 14.5oz (411g) can chopped tomatoes, drained
1 tsp smoked paprika
1 tsp chopped fresh thyme
1 tsp dried oregano
1 bay leaf
1 cup long-grain rice
pinch of saffron threads
3¼ cups chicken stock
2 tbsp tomato paste
2 tbsp fresh lemon juice
salt and freshly ground black pepper
¾ cup frozen peas, rinsed

METHOD

1 Preheat the oven to 350°F (180°C). Heat 1 tbsp of the oil in the casserole dish over high heat. Add the chicken thighs and brown, turning once, about 5 minutes. Transfer the chicken to a plate and set aside.

2 Pour the remaining 1 tbsp oil to the casserole and reduce the heat to medium. Add the onion and cook about 3 minutes, until softened. Stir in the green and red peppers and garlic and cook for 5 minutes, until they soften. Add the tomatoes, smoked paprika, thyme, oregano, and bay leaf, then stir in the rice. Stir for 1–2 minutes.

3 Crumble in the saffron, then stir in the stock, tomato paste, and lemon juice. Season with salt and pepper.

4 Return the chicken thighs to the casserole, nestling them in the rice. Cover and bake for 15 minutes. Add the peas and bake for 10 minutes more, or until the rice is tender and has completely absorbed the cooking liquid. Serve immediately, while still hot.

4 servings

**prep 20 mins
• cook 45 mins**

low fat

**large
flame-proof
casserole**

172

Chicken fricassée

There are many variations of this one-pot French chicken stew.

INGREDIENTS

4 boiling potatoes, peeled and diced
2 tbsp olive oil
4 chicken drumsticks, skin removed
4 chicken thighs, skin removed
salt and freshly ground black pepper
2 tbsp all-purpose flour
4oz (115g) small white mushrooms
4 shallots, sliced
2 garlic cloves, minced
2 tsp chopped rosemary
$^2/_3$ cup dry white wine
$1^1/_4$ cups chicken stock
1 bay leaf

METHOD

1 Cook the potatoes in a saucepan of boiling water for 5 minutes. Drain well.

2 Heat the oil in a large frying pan over medium-high heat. Season the chicken with salt and pepper and dust with the flour. Add to the pan and cook, turning often, about 6 minutes, until browned. Transfer to a plate. Add the shallots to the pan and cook, stirring often, about 2 minutes, until softened. Add the potatoes, mushrooms, garlic, and rosemary, and cook 2 minutes more.

3 Add the wine, bring to a boil, and cook for 1 minute. Add the stock and return to the boil. Return the chicken to the pan, add the bay leaf, and cover. Reduce the heat and simmer about 50 minutes, or until the chicken is very tender. Discard the bay leaf and adjust the seasoning with salt and pepper. Serve hot.

4 servings

**prep 15 mins
• cook 1 hr
15 mins**

low fat

Rabbit Provençale

Rabbit is quite lean, and benefits from braising in an herbed tomato sauce to keep it moist.

INGREDIENTS

2 tbsp olive oil
1 rabbit, 2³⁄₄lb (1.25kg), cut into 10 pieces
4oz (120g) pancetta, diced
1 onion, chopped
4 garlic cloves, finely chopped
2lb (900g) ripe plum tomatoes,
    peeled, seeded, and coarsely chopped
sprig of fresh rosemary, plus more to garnish
3 sage leaves
salt and freshly ground black pepper
²⁄₃ cup dry white wine
³⁄₄ cup boiling water

METHOD

1 Heat the oil in the casserole over medium-high heat. In batches, add the rabbit and cook, turning often, about 5 minutes, or until golden. Transfer to a plate. Pour off all but 1 tbsp of the fat in the casserole.

2 Add the pancetta and onion to the pan and cook for about 5 minutes, stirring, until the pancetta is browned and the onion softened. Add the garlic and stir for about 30 seconds. Add the tomatoes, rosemary, and sage, and season with salt and pepper. Cook for about 10 minutes, stirring often, until the tomatoes give off their juices and they thicken.

3 Stir in the wine, then return the rabbit to the casserole. Cook over medium heat for 20 minutes, or until the liquid has reduced slightly and the sauce is quite thick. Stir in the boiling water. Reduce the heat to low and partially cover. Simmer, stirring occasionally, for about 15 minutes, until the sauce is thick and the rabbit very tender.

4 Remove the pan from the heat and let stand about 10 minutes. Garnish with the rosemary sprigs and serve.

GOOD WITH Boiled new potatoes and broccoli.

4 servings

**prep 15 mins,
plus resting
• cook 1 hr
15 mins**

**large
flame-proof
casserole**

IMPRESS

Bouillabaisse

Originally nothing more than a humble fisherman's soup using the remains of the day's catch, bouillabaisse has evolved into one of the great dishes.

INGREDIENTS

¹/₄ cup olive oil
1 onion, thinly sliced
2 leeks, thinly sliced
1 small fennel bulb, thinly sliced
2–3 garlic cloves, finely chopped
4 tomatoes, skinned, seeded, and chopped
1 cup dry white wine
1 tbsp tomato paste
6 cups hot fish or chicken stock
1 bouquet garni with 1 celery stalk,
   4 thyme springs, and 1 bay leaf
pinch of saffron threads
1 strip of orange zest
1 tbsp chopped parsley
salt and freshly ground pepper

3lb (1.35kg) mixed fish fillets and shellfish, such
   as red snapper, cod, bluefish, clams, mussels,
   and shrimp, prepared as necessary
2 tbsp Pernod (optional)
salt and freshly ground black pepper
8 thin slices day-old French bread,
   toasted, for serving

For the rouille

¹/₂ cup mayonnaise
1 small, fresh hot red chili,
   seeded and roughly chopped
4 garlic cloves, roughly chopped
1 tbsp tomato paste
¹/₂ tsp salt

METHOD

1 Heat the oil in a large saucepan over a medium heat. Add the onion, leeks, fennel, and garlic and cook, stirring frequently, for 5–8 minutes, or until the vegetables are softened but not colored. Add the tomatoes, wine, and tomato paste and stir until blended.

2 Add the stock, bouquet garni, saffron, orange zest, and salt and pepper to taste. Bring to a boil. Reduce the heat, partially cover the pan. Simmer for 30 minutes, or until the soup is reduced slightly, stirring occasionally.

3 To make the rouille, place all ingredients in a food processor and process until smooth. Transfer to a bowl, cover with plastic wrap, and refrigerate until needed.

4 Cut the fish into bite-sized chunks. Remove the orange zest and bouquet garni from the stock, and add the shellfish. Reduce the heat to low and simmer for 3 minutes. Add the fish fillets and simmer for 2–3 minutes more or until the fish flakes easily. Stir in the Pernod, if using, and season with salt and pepper.

5 To serve, spread each piece of toast with rouille and put 2 slices in the bottom of each bowl. Ladle in the soup, including a good selection of fish and shellfish.

GOOD WITH A crisp, dry white wine or a Côtes de Provence rosé. Serve leftover rouille as a spread on a sandwich or as a dip.

PREPARE AHEAD The rouille can be made and chilled for up to 2 days.

4 servings

prep 20 mins
• cook 45 mins

tap the mussels
and discard
any that do
not close

Fisherman's tuna stew

This fish stew, which Basque fisherman call *marmitako de bonito*, was originally made at sea to provide for a hungry crew.

INGREDIENTS

2lb (900g) baking potatoes
1lb 10oz (750g) tuna steaks
12oz (340g) roasted red peppers
3 tbsp olive oil
1 large onion, finely sliced
2 garlic cloves, minced
1 bay leaf
salt and freshly ground black pepper
one 14.5oz (411g) can chopped tomatoes
2 cups frozen baby peas
2 tbsp chopped parsley

METHOD

1 Peel the potatoes and cut into thick rounds. Cut the tuna into pieces roughly the same size as the potatoes. Cut the peppers into strips.

2 Heat the oil in a flame-proof casserole over medium heat. Add the onion, garlic, and bay leaf and cook, stirring often, for about 5 minutes, or until the onions are translucent. Stir in the potatoes. Add cold water to cover and season with salt and pepper. Bring to a boil and cook about 10 minutes, or until the potatoes are almost tender. Add the tomatoes and cook for 5 minutes.

3 Reduce the heat to medium-low. Add the tuna and cook for 5 minutes. Add the peas and pepper strips and simmer for 10 minutes. Sprinkle with parsley. Ladle into soup bowls and serve hot.

4 servings

prep 10 mins
• cook 35 mins

Mediterranean lasagna

A simple baked vegetarian pasta dish full of Italian flavors.

INGREDIENTS

4 small eggplants
salt and freshly ground black pepper
1 large red bell pepper
4 large portabella mushrooms, stemmed
olive oil, for the dish
4 cups marinara sauce
8oz (227g) oven-ready lasagna
1lb (450g) mozzarella cheese, thinly sliced
15oz (420g) ricotta cheese
1/4 cup freshly grated Parmesan

METHOD

1 Cut the eggplants lengthwise 1/2in (13mm) thick. Place in a colander on a plate and toss with 1 1/2 tbsp of salt. Let stand 30–60 minutes to draw out the bitter juices. Rinse well and pat dry with paper towels.

2 Position an oiled broiler rack 6in (15cm) from the heat and preheat the broiler. Broil the eggplant, peppers, and mushrooms for 5–10 minutes, or until they are softened but still hold their shape. Season to taste with salt and pepper.

3 Preheat the oven to 375°F (190°C). Lightly oil the baking dish and spoon in a spoonful of the marinara sauce. Top with a layer of pasta, some vegetables, another spoonful of sauce, then some of the mozzarella and ricotta. Repeat the layers, finishing with tomato sauce, topped with some vegetables. Sprinkle with the Parmesan.

4 Cover the dish tightly with aluminium foil and place on a baking sheet. Bake for 30 minutes. Remove the foil and bake for 15 minutes more to brown the top. Remove from the oven and let stand 15 minutes before serving.

8 servings

**prep 20 mins
• cook 1 hr
10 mins**

**9 x 13in
(23 x 33cm)
baking dish**

Vegetable moussaka

Lentils replace the lamb, and yogurt is a light alternative to béchamel sauce, in this vegetarian version of a Greek favorite.

INGREDIENTS

2 medium eggplants, about 24oz (70g), cut into ½in (13mm) slices

2 zucchini, cut into ½in (13mm) slices

2 onions, cut into ½in (13mm) half-moons

2 red bell peppers, seeded and cut into ½in (13mm) wide strips

4 tbsp olive oil

salt and freshly ground black pepper

2 garlic cloves, chopped

1 tbsp chopped thyme

one 14.5oz (411g) can chopped tomatoes

one 15oz (420g) can lentils, drained and rinsed

2 tbsp chopped parsley

1¼ cups Greek-style yogurt

2 large eggs, lightly beaten

pinch of paprika

3oz (85g) feta cheese, crumbled

2 tbsp sesame seeds

METHOD

1 Preheat the oven to 425°F (220°C). Toss the eggplant, zucchini, onions, and red peppers in a roasting pan. Drizzle with the oil and toss. Season with salt and pepper.

2 Roast for 10 minutes. Stir in the garlic and thyme. Continue roasting for 30–35 minutes, or until the vegetables are tender. Reduce the temperature to 350°F (180°C).

3 Stir the tomatoes with their juices, the lentils, and the parsley into the roasted vegetables and season with salt and pepper. Transfer the vegetables to a 9in (23cm) square baking dish.

4 Beat the yogurt, eggs, and paprika together and season lightly with salt and pepper (keeping in mind that the feta cheese is very salty). Spread over the vegetables and sprinkle with the feta. Place on a baking sheet and bake for 40 minutes. Sprinkle with the sesame seeds and bake for 10 minutes more, or until the top is golden brown. Let stand 5 minutes, then serve hot (or cool and serve at room temperature).

GOOD WITH A mixed green salad and crusty rustic bread.

4–6 servings

**prep 20 mins
• cook 1½ hrs**

Seafood paella

This Spanish rice dish has many regional variations. This version contains a delicious mix of seafood.

INGREDIENTS

5 tbsp olive oil
12 jumbo shrimp, peeled and deveined
8 langoustines or more shrimp
8oz (225g) squid, cleaned and sliced into rings
12–16 mussels, scrubbed
2 large tomatoes, peeled, seeded, and diced
pinch of saffron
2 cups short-grain rice
5 cups boiling fish stock
salt and freshly ground black pepper
2 tbsp chopped parsley
1 lemon, cut into 8 wedges

METHOD

1 Heat 2 tbsp of the oil in a paella pan or a large frying pan over medium heat. Add the shrimp and cook about 2 minutes. Transfer to a plate. Add the langoustines to the pan, cover, and cook for 5 minutes, until the shells are red. Add to the shrimp. Add 1 tbsp oil to the pan, heat, and add the squid. Cook 1 minute, until barely opaque, and add to the plate. Add the mussels to the pan with ¼ cup water. Cover and cook about 4 minutes, or until they open. Transfer mussels and their juices to the plate.

2 Heat 2 tbsp oil in the pan. Add the tomatoes and saffron and cook for 1 minute. Stir in the rice, then the stock.

3 Simmer, uncovered, over medium-low heat for 15 minutes. Season with salt and pepper to taste. Nestle the shrimp, langoustines, squid, and mussels in the rice and let cook until the rice is just tender.

4 Remove from the heat and tent with aluminum foil. Let stand for 5 minutes. Garnish with the lemon and parsley and serve hot.

4 servings

**prep 10 mins
• cook 30 mins**

**tap the mussels
and discard
any that do
not close**

Mussels in white wine sauce

Cooking in wine, garlic, and herbs is one of the easiest ways to prepare mussels, and one of the best.

INGREDIENTS
4 tbsp butter
2 onions, finely chopped
8lb (3.6kg) mussels, cleaned
2¼ cups dry white wine
2 garlic cloves, minced
4 bay leaves
2 sprigs thyme
salt and freshly ground black pepper
2–4 tbsp chopped parsley

METHOD
1 Melt the butter in a soup pot over medium heat. Add the onion and cook about 6 minutes, until lightly browned. Add the mussels, wine, garlic, bay leaves, and thyme, and season with salt and pepper. Cover and bring to a boil over high heat. Cook, shaking the pan often, for about 6 minutes, or until the mussels have opened.

2 Transfer the mussels to large serving bowls, discarding any mussels that do not open. Cover the bowls with a large clean kitchen towel to keep the mussels warm.

3 Strain the liquid through a fine sieve into a saucepan and bring to a boil over high heat. Add the parsley and adjust the seasoning. Pour the sauce over the mussels and serve immediately.

GOOD WITH Plenty of French bread for sopping up the juices.

4 servings

prep 20 mins
• cook 10 mins

tap the mussels
and discard
any that do
not close

Spicy shrimp gratin

Shrimp is covered with cheese sauce and broiled until golden.

INGREDIENTS
1½lb (675g) large shrimp, peeled and deveined
juice of 2 limes
few drops of hot red pepper sauce
2 tbsp olive oil
2 red onions, finely sliced
3 fresh hot red chilies, seeded and minced
3 garlic cloves, minced
salt and freshly ground black pepper
1 cup heavy cream
¾ cup shredded Gruyère

METHOD
1 Toss the shrimp, lime juice, and hot pepper sauce in a bowl and let stand for about 15 minutes.

2 Position the broiler rack about 8 inches from the source of heat and preheat the broiler. Heat the oil in a large frying pan over medium heat. Add the onions and cook, stirring occasionally, about 5 minutes, until softened. Add the chilies and garlic and cook about 5 minutes more, until tender.

3 Spread in the large, oven-proof serving dish. Drain the shrimp and arrange over the onions. Season with salt and pepper. Pour in the cream, sprinkle with the Gruyère.

4 Broil about 5 minutes, or until the shrimp turn opaque and the cheese is golden. Serve at once.

GOOD WITH Fresh bread and a crisp green salad.

6 servings

prep 10 mins,
plus marinating
• cook 15–16 mins

large
flame-proof
serving dish

Fish in coconut stew

This is a popular Brazilian stew, rich with creamy coconut milk. An authentic ingredient is palm oil (*dendê*), which lends a distinctive flavor and color, but you can use more olive oil instead.

INGREDIENTS

4 tbsp olive oil

1 onion, thinly sliced

3 ripe tomatoes, skinned, seeded, and chopped

1 red bell pepper, seeded and thinly sliced

1 green bell pepper, seeded and thinly sliced

1 cup canned coconut milk

1 tbsp tomato paste

salt and freshly ground black pepper

1³⁄₄lb (800g) firm white fish, such as cod or snapper, cut into large chunks or strips

3 tbsp palm oil (optional)

1 tbsp chopped cilantro

For the salsa

1 ripe tomato, skinned, seeded, and chopped

1 small red onion, finely chopped

1 garlic clove, finely chopped

1 tbsp red wine vinegar

1 tbsp fresh lime juice

1 tbsp vegetable oil

1 tbsp chopped parsley

1 tsp hot pepper sauce

METHOD

1 Heat the olive oil in a deep frying pan over medium heat. Add the onion and cook, stirring frequently, for 5 minutes, until tender but not browned. Add the tomatoes and the peppers. Reduce the heat to medium-low and simmer, stirring occasionally, for 20 minutes, until the vegetables have softened and released their juices. Stir in the coconut milk and tomato paste and return to a boil. Season with salt and pepper.

2 Meanwhile, make the salsa. Mix all the ingredients together and spoon into a serving bowl. Set aside to allow the flavors to blend.

3 Add the fish to the coconut milk mixture and cook, stirring occasionally, for 7 minutes, until the fish is opaque throughout. Do not overcook. Stir in the palm oil, if using.

4 Transfer the stew to a heated serving dish and sprinkle with the cilantro. Serve hot, with the salsa passed on the side.

GOOD WITH Boiled white rice.

PREPARE AHEAD Prepare, cool, and refrigerate the stew up through step 1 up to 1 day ahead. When ready to serve, heat and add the fish. The salsa can be made up to 1 day ahead, but stir in the chopped parsley at the last minute.

4 servings

prep 15 mins
• cook 35 mins

Salt cod braised with vegetables

Here, salt cod (*bacalao*) is simmered with the fragrant Spanish aromas of garlic, bay, and saffron to a lovely tenderness.

INGREDIENTS

3 tbsp olive oil
1 onion, finely diced
2 leeks, white part only, finely sliced
3 ripe tomatoes, peeled, seeded, and chopped
3 garlic cloves, minced
18oz (500g) baking potatoes, peeled and diced
generous pinch of saffron
2 bay leaves
salt and freshly ground black pepper
1¾lb (800g) thick-cut salt cod,
    soaked, drained, and cut into 4 pieces
½ cup dry white wine
2 tbsp chopped parsley

METHOD

1 Heat the oil in a large, shallow flame-proof casserole over medium-low heat. Add the onion and leek and cook, stirring often, about 5 minutes, until tender.

2 Stir in the tomatoes and garlic and cook for 2 minutes. Add the potatoes, saffron, and bay leaves, and season well with salt and pepper.

3 Place the salt cod, skin side up, on the vegetables. Pour in the wine and 1 cup water. Bring to a simmer. Cook, shaking the casserole every 5 minutes or so to release gelatin from the fish to thicken the sauce, for about 25 minutes, or until the potatoes are tender.

4 Sprinkle with parsley and serve hot, from the casserole.

4 servings

prep 20 mins, plus soaking • cook 40 mins

soak the fish for at least 24 hrs in enough water to cover, changing the water 2–3 times to remove salt

Mussels with spicy tomato sauce

The distinctly Spanish flavor of smoked paprika is a welcome addition to the classic mussels in tomato sauce.

INGREDIENTS

2 tbsp extra virgin olive oil
2 tbsp butter
2 shallots, finely chopped
1 celery stalk, finely chopped
1 garlic clove, minced
1 fresh hot red chili, seeded and minced
½ tsp smoked paprika
4lb (1.8kg) mussels, cleaned
2 large ripe tomatoes, chopped
½ cup dry white wine
2 tbsp chopped parsley

METHOD

1 Heat the oil and butter in a large soup pot with lid over low heat. Add the shallots, celery, garlic, and chili and cook until the shallots have softened. Stir in the paprika.

2 Add the mussels, tomatoes, and wine and stir well. Increase the heat to medium-high and bring to a boil. Cover and cook, shaking the pan often, for about 6 minutes, or until the mussels open.

3 Transfer the mussels to deep serving bowls and sprinkle with parsley. Serve hot.

GOOD WITH Slices of warm crusty bread to mop up the rich juices.

4 servings

**prep 15 mins
• cook 10 mins**

**tap the mussels
and discard
any that do
not close**

Baked porgy

This Spanish dish works well with many whole fish, such as porgy (as shown here), snapper, or trout.

INGREDIENTS

2 porgy, about 21oz (600g) each
2 tbsp tapenade, preferably homemade
1 lemon
3 tbsp olive oil
1½lb (675g) red-skinned potatoes,
    very thinly sliced
1 onion, thinly sliced
2 red or green bell peppers,
    seeded and sliced into thin rings
4 garlic cloves, chopped
2 tbsp chopped parsley
1 tsp hot smoked paprika
½ cup dry white wine
salt and freshly ground black pepper

METHOD

1 Make 2 parallel diagonal cuts in the thickest parts on each side of each fish. Place in a nonmetallic dish and spread the tapenade over the inside and outside of the fish. Cut 2 slices of the lemon. Tuck a lemon slice into each fish and squeeze the juice from the remaining lemon over the top. Cover and refrigerate for at least 1 and up to 2 hours.

2 Preheat the oven to 375°F (190°C). Coat an oven-proof dish with 1 tbsp of the oil. Layer half the potatoes in the dish. Layer the onions and peppers on top, sprinkle with the garlic and parsley, sprinkle with the paprika, then top with the remaining potatoes. Drizzle the remaining oil over the potatoes and sprinkle with 3 tbsp water. Cover with aluminum foil. Bake for 40 minutes.

3 Increase the oven to 425°F (220°C). Place the fish on top of the potatoes, pour the wine over the fish, and season well with salt and pepper. Return the dish to the oven, uncovered, for 20 minutes, until the fish is opaque when pierced with a knife. Serve immediately.

PREPARE AHEAD The fish can be prepared to the end of step 1 up to 6 hours in advance.

4 servings

prep 10 mins,
plus marinating
• cook 1 hr

Lobster thermidor

This irresistibly indulgent seafood dish is thought to be named in honor of the play *Thermidor*, which opened in 1894 in Paris.

INGREDIENTS
2 cooked lobsters, 1½lb (675g) each

For the sauce
2 tbsp butter
2 shallots, finely chopped
½ cup dry white wine
⅔ cup heavy cream
½ cup fish stock
2 tbsp chopped parsley
2 tsp chopped tarragon
1 tbsp fresh lemon juice
½ tsp dry mustard
¾ cup shredded Gruyère
salt and freshly ground black pepper
sweet paprika, for garnish
lemon wedges, for serving

METHOD
1 Cut the lobsters in half lengthwise. Remove the meat from the claws and tail, along with any coral or meat from the head. Cut the lobster meat into bite-sized pieces. Clean out the body shells and reserve.

2 To prepare the sauce, melt the butter in a small saucepan over medium-low heat. Add the shallots and cook about 2 minutes, until softened. Add the wine and boil for 2–3 minutes to reduce the liquid by about half.

3 Add the cream and stock and boil rapidly, stirring often, about 7 minutes, until reduced and beginning to thicken. Stir in the parsley, tarragon, lemon juice, and mustard. Stir in half of the Gruyère. Season with salt and pepper.

4 Preheat the broiler. Add the lobster meat to the sauce, then divide between the lobster shells. Sprinkle the remaining cheese over the top.

5 Place on a foil-lined broiler rack. Broil for 2–3 minutes, until bubbling and golden. Sprinkle with a little paprika. Serve hot, with lemon wedges.

4 servings

prep 25 mins
• cook 20 mins

Chicken gumbo

This hearty soup-stew from Cajun country will have the richest flavor if you use chicken thigh meat.

INGREDIENTS

1 tbsp vegetable oil
1 onion, chopped
2 celery ribs, chopped
1 green bell pepper, seeded and chopped
1 garlic clove, chopped
1lb (450g) boneless and skinless chicken thighs, cubed
2 tsp sweet or hot paprika
$\frac{1}{2}$ tsp dried oregano
$\frac{1}{2}$ tsp ground cumin
1 tbsp all-purpose flour
2 cups chicken stock
one 14.5oz (411g) can chopped tomatoes
4oz (115g) andouille or kielbasa sausage, sliced
8oz (225g) frozen sliced okra
salt and freshly ground black pepper

METHOD

1 Heat the oil in a large saucepan over medium heat. Add the onion, celery, and green pepper and cook for 5 minutes, stirring often, until softened. Stir in the garlic.

2 Add the chicken and cook, turning frequently, about 10 minutes, or until just browned. Stir in the paprika, oregano, cumin, and flour. Stir for 1 minute, then stir in the stock, tomatoes, and sausage.

3 Boil, then reduce the heat and simmer for 20 minutes. Add the okra and simmer for 20 minutes, until the chicken is tender. Season with salt and pepper and serve hot.

4 servings

prep 20 mins
• cook 50 mins

Grilled quail with ginger glaze

These quail have a sweet and sour southeast Asian style. Cook them on a grill, under a broiler, or on a hot griddle pan.

INGREDIENTS
8 quail
lime wedges, to serve

For the marinade
3 tbsp sweet chili dipping sauce
3 tbsp finely chopped cilantro
2 tbsp fresh lime juice
1 tbsp Asian sesame oil
1 garlic clove, crushed
one $\frac{1}{2}$in (13mm) piece peeled and finely grated fresh ginger
1 garlic clove, crushed through a press

METHOD
1 Using poultry shears or strong scissors, cut each quail down one side of the backbone. Open the quail and place on a work surface, skin side up. Press each quail firmly on the breastbone to flatten. Slash the breast skin with a knife.

2 Mix the marinade ingredients in a small bowl. Place the quail in a nonmetallic dish. Brush the marinade over the quail, especially in the cuts. Cover and refrigerate for 1 hour–2 days.

3 Position the broiler rack 6in (15cm) from the source of heat and preheat the broiler. Line a broiler pan with oiled aluminum foil and place the quail on the pan. Broil for 12–15 minutes, turning once, until golden brown and the juices show no trace of pink when pierced at the bone with the tip of a sharp knife.

4 Serve hot, with lime wedges for squeezing.

GOOD WITH Boiled rice and green vegetables, such as French beans.

4 servings

prep 15 mins, plus marinating • cook 15 mins

the quail and marinade can be frozen for 1 month

Beef stroganoff

This classic Russian dish was named after the Strogonov family.

INGREDIENTS
2 tbsp butter
1 onion, thinly sliced
8oz (225g) cremini mushrooms, sliced
1½lb (675g) filet mignon,
    cut across the grain into
    2 x ½in (5 x 13mm) strips
salt and freshly ground black pepper
3 tbsp all-purpose flour
1 tbsp sweet paprika, plus extra for sprinkling
2 tbsp olive oil
1¼ cups sour cream or crème fraîche
1 tbsp Dijon mustard
2 tbsp fresh lemon juice

METHOD
1 Heat the butter in a large frying pan over medium heat. Add the onion and cook about 8 minutes, until golden. Add the mushrooms and cook about 5 minutes, until they begin to brown. Transfer to a plate.

2 Meanwhile, season the beef with salt and pepper. Mix the flour and paprika together in a large bowl, add the beef and toss well. Add the oil to the pan and increase the heat to high. In batches, add the beef and cook, stirring occasionally, for about 3 minutes, until the meat is seared. Transfer to a plate.

3 Return the beef, onions, and mushrooms to the pan. Stir over high heat for 1 minute. Reduce the heat to medium-low. Stir in the sour cream and mustard and heat, but do not boil.

4 Stir in the lemon juice and season with salt and pepper. Sprinkle with paprika and serve hot.

GOOD WITH Rice or egg noodles.

4 servings

prep 15 mins
• cook 25 mins

Beef daube with wild mushrooms

This stew is redolent with red wine and earthy mushrooms.

INGREDIENTS
2 tbsp olive oil
2 tbsp butter
2lb (900g) beef chuck,
    cut into 3in (7.5cm) pieces
salt and freshly ground pepper
2 tbsp all-purpose flour
4oz (115g) pancetta, chopped
1 large onion, finely chopped
1 celery stalk, finely chopped
3 garlic cloves, minced
3 carrots, diced
1 tbsp chopped thyme
one 750ml bottle hearty red wine
zest and juice of 1 orange
2 tbsp brandy (optional)
1 tbsp tomato paste
1oz (30g) dried porcini mushrooms
6oz (175g) cremini mushrooms, sliced

METHOD

1 Heat the olive oil and butter in the casserole over medium-high heat. Season the beef with salt and pepper. Toss the beef in the flour. In batches, add to the casserole. Cook, turning occasionally, about 5 minutes, until browned. Transfer to a plate.

2 Add the pancetta, onion, celery, bacon, and garlic to the casserole and cook about 7 minutes, until lightly colored. Return the beef to the casserole and add the carrots and thyme. Pour in the wine, the orange zest and juice, brandy, if using, and the tomato paste. Bring to a boil. Reduce the heat to low and cover. Simmer for 1 hour.

3 Soak the dried mushrooms in hot tap water to cover about 30 minutes, until softened. Drain well and chop the mushrooms. Add the soaked and fresh mushrooms to the casserole and continue cooking until the beef is very tender, about 1 hour longer. Serve hot.

GOOD WITH Buttered egg noodles or parsleyed boiled potatoes.

4–6 servings

prep 30 mins
• cook 2½ hrs

large flame-proof
casserole with
a tight-fitting lid

freeze for up to
3 months

Veal scaloppine

This popular Italian dish uses a classic method to prepare veal.

INGREDIENTS

1/2 cup all-purpose flour
salt and freshly ground black pepper
4 veal cutlet, about 6oz (180g) each, patted dry
4 tbsp butter
2 tbsp olive oil
1/4 cup dry white wine
1 cup veal or chicken stock
2 tbsp chopped parsley
lemon wedges, to serve

METHOD

1 Preheat the oven to 200°F (100°C). Season the flour with salt and pepper to taste. One at a time, put a veal cutlet between 2 sheets of wax paper and pound with a rolling pin until very thin. Coat the veal on both sides with the flour, then shake off the excess; set aside.

2 Melt 1½ tbsp of the butter with the oil in a large frying pan over medium heat until sizzling. Add 2 cutlets and cook for 1–2 minutes on each side, pressing down firmly with a spatula to keep the meat as flat as possible, until golden. Transfer the veal to a plate and keep warm in the oven. Repeat with the remaining veal, adding 1½ tbsp butter to the frying pan.

3 Add the wine to the pan, increase the heat, and let boil for about 1 minute. Add the stock and any juices from the plate of veal and continue boiling until the liquid is reduced by half. Stir in the parsley, remaining butter, and salt and pepper to taste.

4 Place the veal on dinner plates and top with the pan juices. Serve at once with lemon wedges for squeezing over the veal.

GOOD WITH Sautéed spinach or a green salad. Leftovers are delicious served cold: try slicing into strips and mixing with a tossed salad and dressing.

PREPARE AHEAD The veal can be pounded in advance and refrigerated until required.

4 servings

prep 10 mins
• cook 8 mins

Choucroute garni

This is a simpler, quicker version of a classic dish from Alsace.

INGREDIENTS

3 tbsp rendered duck fat or vegetable oil
9oz (250g) ham steak, diced, bone discarded
1½lb (674g) pork spareribs, cut into ribs
2 onions, chopped
2 Granny Smith apples, peeled, cored, and sliced
1 garlic clove, minced
6 whole black peppercorns, lightly crushed
6 juniper berries, lightly crushed
large sprig of thyme
2 bay leaves
2lb (900g) fresh sauerkraut,
    thoroughly rinsed and drained
2 cups chicken stock
1¼ cups lager beer or Riesling wine
12 small new potatoes, scrubbed
1lb (450g) smoked sausage, such as bratwurst,
    cut into 6 portions
salt and freshly ground black pepper
chopped parsley, to garnish

METHOD

1 Heat 2 tbsp of the fat in the casserole over medium heat. In batches, add the ham and spareribs and cook, turning occasionally, about 5 minutes, until browned. Transfer to a plate. Add the onion to the casserole and cook until softened, about 3 minutes.

2 Add the apples, garlic, peppercorns, juniper berries, thyme, and bay leaves. Stir in the sauerkraut. Return the ham and spareribs to the casserole and stir in the stock and beer or wine. Bring to a simmer. Cover tightly and reduce the heat to low. Simmer for 2 hours.

3 Add the potatoes, pushing them into the sauerkraut, then cover and continue cooking for about 50 minutes, or until the potatoes are tender. Season with salt and pepper.

4 Meanwhile, heat the remaining 1 tbsp fat in a frying pan over medium heat. Add the sausage and cook, turning, about 5 minutes, until browned.

5 Spoon onto a platter and arrange the sausages on top. Sprinkle with parsley and serve hot.

GOOD WITH Hot mustard or horseradish on the side, and a glass of cold beer or Riesling.

6–8 servings

prep 30 mins
• cook 3 hrs

large
flame-proof
casserole

Osso bucco

Veal shanks have a richness unlike any other cut of meat and turn this stew into an extraordinary meal.

INGREDIENTS

four 1½in (4cm) thick veal shanks
salt and freshly ground black pepper
¼ cup all-purpose flour
2 tbsp butter
2 tbsp olive oil
1 small onion, chopped
4 garlic cloves, chopped
½ cup beef stock or water, as needed
¼ cup tomato paste
3 tbsp chopped parsley
2 anchovy fillets in oil, minced
grated zest of 1 lemon

METHOD

1 Season the veal with salt and pepper. Dredge in the flour and shake off any excess.

2 Melt the butter with the oil in the casserole over medium-high heat. Add the veal and cook, turning occasionally, about 5 minutes, or until browned all over. Transfer to a plate. Add the onion and garlic to the casserole and reduce the heat to medium-low. Cook, stirring occasionally, for 5 minutes or until softened but not colored.

3 Stir in the stock and tomato paste, season with salt and pepper, and bring to a boil. Return the veal to the casserole. Reduce the heat to low and cover. Simmer for 1½ hours or until the veal is tender. Check the stew occasionally, and if the cooking liquid has reduced too much, add more stock. The finished cooking liquid should be thick.

4 Stir the parsley, anchovies, and lemon zest into the casserole. Adjust the seasoning as required and serve immediately.

GOOD WITH A saffron-flavored risotto or cooked long-grain rice.

PREPARE AHEAD The stew can be cooked, then chilled for up to 2 days. Reheat gently, then complete step 4.

4 servings

**prep 15 mins
• cook 1¾ hrs**

**hind shanks
make the
best, meatiest
osso bucco**

**large flame-
proof casserole**

**complete steps
1–3, then cool
and freeze for
up to 1 month.
Thaw completely,
then reheat and
complete step 4**

Spanish bean and pork stew

Known in Spain as *fabada*, this rib-sticking stew is quickly made with canned beans. Use your favorite sausages as you prefer.

INGREDIENTS

9oz (250g) chorizo or andouille
9oz (250g) morcilla (Spanish blood sausage)
  or garlic sausage
9oz (250g) slab bacon or pancetta, rind removed
1 tbsp olive oil
¼ cup hearty red wine
two 15oz (420g) cans white kidney (cannellini) beans,
  drained and rinsed
pinch of saffron threads
1 bay leaf
2 cups chicken stock

METHOD

1 Cut the sausages and bacon into 2in (5cm) chunks. Heat the oil in a large casserole over medium-low heat. Add the sausages and bacon, and cook, stirring occasionally, for about 3 minutes. Increase the heat and pour in the wine. Boil about 2 minutes, until reduced by half.

2 Stir in the beans, saffron, and bay leaf, then enough chicken stock to barely cover. Bring to a boil, reduce the heat, cover, and simmer for 30 minutes. Serve hot.

GOOD WITH Crusty bread.

4 servings

prep 5 mins
• cook 40 mins

Autumn game casserole

Mixed game makes a wonderfully rich-flavored dish. Use chunks of boneless and skinless turkey or pork loin as a substitute.

INGREDIENTS

2 tbsp olive oil
18oz (500g) mixed boneless and skinless game,
   such as pheasant, partridge, venison, rabbit,
   and pigeon, diced
1 onion, sliced
1 carrot, sliced
1 parsnip, sliced
1 fennel bulb, sliced, fronds reserved
2 tbsp all-purpose flour
1 cup chicken stock
$^3/_4$ cup hard apple cider or apple juice
9oz (250g) cremini mushrooms, thickly sliced
$^1/_2$ tsp fennel seeds
salt and freshly ground black pepper

METHOD

1 Preheat the oven to 325°F (160°C). Heat 1 tbsp of the oil in the casserole over medium-high heat. Add the game and cook for 3–4 minutes, stirring occasionally, until lightly browned. Transfer to a plate.

2 Add the remaining oil to the pot and heat. Add the onion, carrot, parsnip, and fennel and cook for 4–5 minutes, stirring occasionally, until lightly colored. Sprinkle in the flour and stir. Gradually stir in the stock and cider. Add the mushrooms and fennel seeds, then return the meat to the pan.

3 Season with salt and pepper and bring to a boil. Cover and bake for about $1^1/_2$ hours, or until the meat is tender.

4 Sprinkle the casserole with the reserved fennel fronds and serve hot.

PREPARE AHEAD The casserole can be cooked, cooled, and refrigerated for up to 2 days, and will improve in flavor during that time.

4 servings

prep 20 mins
• cook 1 hr
30 mins

flame-proof
casserole

freeze for up
to 3 months

INDEX

Page numbers in *italics* indicate
illustrations.

ACKNOWLEDGMENTS

DORLING KINDERSLEY WOULD LIKE TO THANK THE FOLLOWING:

Photographers
Steve Baxter, Martin Brigdale, Tony Cambio, Nigel Gibson, Francesco Guillamet,
Adrian Heapy, Jeff Kauck, David Munns, David Murray, Ian O'Leary, Roddy Paine,
William Reavell, Gavin Sawyer, William Shaw, Carole Tuff, Kieran Watson,
Stuart West, Jon Whitaker

Prop Stylist
Sue Rowlands

Food Stylist
Jennifer White

Picture Research
Emma Shepherd

Index
Susan Bosanko

Useful information

Refrigerator and freezer storage guidelines

FOOD	REFRIGERATOR	FREEZER
Raw poultry, fish, and meat (small pieces)	2–3 days	3–6 months
Raw minced beef and poultry	1–2 days	3 months
Cooked whole roasts or whole poultry	2–3 days	9 months
Cooked poultry pieces	1–2 days	1 month (6 months in stock or gravy)
Soups and stews	2–3 days	1–3 months
Casseroles	2–3 days	2–4 weeks

Oven temperature equivalents

FAHRENHEIT	CELSIUS	DESCRIPTION
225°F	110°C	Cool
250°F	130°C	Cool
275°F	140°C	Very low
300°F	150°C	Very low
325°F	160°C	Low
350°F	180°C	Moderate
375°F	190°C	Moderately hot
400°F	200°C	Hot
425°F	220°C	Hot
450°F	230°C	Very hot
475°F	240°C	Very hot